Chalcedonian No More

A Reformed Critique of the Barthian
Christology of Bruce L. McCormack

Michael L. Aiken

CHALCEDONIAN
NO MORE

**A Reformed Critique of the Barthian
Christology of Bruce L. McCormack**

Michael L. Aiken

Chalcedonian No More:
A Reformed Critique of the Barthian Christology of Bruce L. McCormack
By Michael L. Aiken

A thesis submitted to the faculty of *Westminster Theological Seminary* in partial fulfillment of the requirements for the degree Masters of Theology 2015.

Faculty Advisor: Dr. K Scott Oliphint
Second Faculty Reader: Dr. Lane G. Tipton
Chairman of the Field Committee: Dr. Lane G. Tipton
Librarian: Mr. Alexander (Sandy) Finlayson

Graduation date: May 2015

Michael Aiken may be reached at mcaiken1@msn.com.

Cover and interior design: Benjamin Vrbicek
Cover image: Council of Chalcedon fresco in the Vatican Library
    (www.encyclopediaurantia.org/images/BOL120.JPG)

First printing December 2015

ISBN-13: 978-1522871163
ISBN-10: 1522871160

Special thanks to Mary Wells for her editorial assistance and to James Cassidy for his theological assistance.

CONTENTS

INTRODUCTION

In recent discussions, Karl Barth's Christology has been described as "Chalcedonian."[1] These discussions are both challenging and stimulating to the church's understanding of Christology and afford an opportunity to sharpen its understanding of the Bible's teaching on Christ's person. Since it is generally agreed that the creed of Chalcedon defines orthodox Christology, our concern in this thesis is to explore whether the Christology of Karl Barth is Chalcedonian. This study will examine the interpretation of Barthian Christology in the proposal of Bruce L. McCormack. Specifically, it will focus on four areas as they relate to the person of Christ: (1) the ground of Christ's deity (theological ontology), (2) one person Christology, (3) two natures in Christ, and (4) divine immutability.

Barth, according to McCormack, was critical of the christological tradition of Chalcedon and believed its view of God's essence as absolute and complete in himself was inconsistent with its belief in divine immutability and

---

[1] See Bruce L. McCormack, *Orthodox and Modern: Studies in the Theology of Karl Barth* (Grand Rapids: Baker Academic, 2008), 201; and George Hunsinger "Karl Barth's Christology: Its Basic Chalcedonian Character," in *The Cambridge Companion to Karl Barth*, ed. John Webster (Cambridge: Cambridge University Press, 2000), 127-42.

2 CHALCEDONIAN NO MORE

impassibility as it relates to the incarnation of the Logos.[2] He believed these doctrines originated from Greek philosophy and rendered the Christology of the Chalcedonian fathers incoherent.[3] We will examine whether McCormack's argument for what he calls "an actualized theological ontology" is consistent and compatible with the Reformed tradition of Chalcedon. In other words, is it possible to synthesize an actualized ontology with the Chalcedonian explanation of Christology and still be orthodox? In the end we will see that McCormack's proposal is opposed to the Reformed tradition of Chalcedon. We hope as well to argue that the church, as it faces the new challenges of modernism, needs to continue to adhere to the Christology of Scripture, as expressed in the Chalcedonian creed.

---

[2] McCormack, *Orthodox and Modern*, 205, 209.
[3] Ibid., 188.

CHAPTER 1

KARL BARTH AND THE CHRISTOLOGY OF BRUCE MCCORMACK

Our concern in this chapter centers on Bruce L. McCormack's Barthian proposal of Christology rather than a direct investigation of Barth himself. I have chosen McCormack because his entire career has passionately and consistently advanced the theology of Karl Barth for the Christian church in order to sharpen and advance its theology. McCormack consistently beckons Evangelicals, and even the Reformed, to include the Swiss theologian as a theological partner of conversation. For instance, when confronted with the liberal challenges to penal substitution, McCormack offers this advice to Evangelicals:

> Indeed, an adequate response would require that penal substitution be integrated not only into a well-ordered Christology, but into a well-ordered doctrine of the Trinity as well. And this means entering into questions of theological ontology with the same degree of rigor that the early church leaders displayed. *It is precisely here that I think Karl Barth offers a great deal of help*. I do not mean to suggest that he is the only possible resource that Evangelicals could turn to

when confronted by the current moral challenge to penal substitution. *But I do think that he is the best.*[4]

McCormack criticizes Evangelicals for showing little interest in divine ontology. [5] His proposal is for the Christian church to consider seriously the actualized theological ontology of Karl Barth as the answer to old, and new, theological problems. In this chapter, we will be looking at the details of McCormack's christological proposal to understand its uniqueness in relation to the Chalcedonian creed. By exploring McCormack's Christology, we will see that his understanding of God's being (Barth's theological ontology) is different than that of the Chalcedonian fathers.

PRELIMINARY CONSIDERATIONS

What is the Christology of Karl Barth according to Bruce L. McCormack? We will see that it is Chalcedonian but with qualifications. It is described as a "historicized" Christology. When commenting on the characterization of the "historicized Chalcedonianism" of Barth's Christology, McCormack explains,

By this I meant that Barth's later Christology preserves all the theological values resident in the

[4] Bruce L. McCormack, "The Ontological Presuppositions of Barth's Doctrine of the Atonement," in *The Glory of the Atonement: Biblical, Theological and Practical Perspectives*, ed. Charles E. Hill and Frank A. James III (Downers Grove, IL: Inter Varsity Press, 2004), 348 (emphasis mine).

[5] Ibid., 346. In commenting on what McCormack perceived as the weakness of the approach to systematic theology at Covenant Seminary, he states that "There was a decided lack of interest in 'ontological' questions within the realm of dogmatics." McCormack sees this weakness going back to the Reformation.

Chalcedonian formula and is, to this extent, faithful to the witness of that formula. That much I can certainly still say. But the question I wish to pose here…is whether Barth's later Christology does not so much constitute a revision of the meaning of the terms employed in the formula as it does the substitution of *an altogether different ontology* which makes continued use of the term "Chalcedonian" misleading as applied to him.[6]

As we can see, the Barthian Christology of Bruce McCormack will have a different understanding of God's essence (ontology) and also a different terminology than the Chalcedonian fathers, all the while retaining the "theological values" of the creed. Also important to note is the close connection between Barth's theological ontology and the meaning of the terms he uses to describe Christ's person.

We will structure our exploration of McCormack by focusing on his essay entitled "Karl Barth's Historicized Christology: Just How 'Chalcedonian' Is It?"[7] McCormack begins by stating how a number of Barth scholars have claimed Barth is Chalcedonian. He wants to test the validity of that claim.[8] His contention is that Barth's Christology, found in *Church Dogmatics* (hereafter, *CD*) I/2, is more Chalcedonian than his later writings, especially from *CD* II/2 onward.[9] *CD* II/2 is where Barth reworks his doctrine of election and is in clear opposition to Calvin and Reformed orthodoxy.[10] Barth's actualistic theological ontology is the key difference between the earlier Barth of *CD* I/2 and the later Barth from *CD* II/2 and beyond. In *CD* I/2, Barth slips into a Greek metaphysical ontology of

---

[6] McCormack, *Orthodox and Modern*, 201 (emphasis mine).

[7] In ibid., 201-33.

[8] Ibid., 201.

[9] Ibid., 201-2.

[10] Ibid., 202, 189.

God's being and is not "thoroughly" actualistic. Specifically, actualism is seen in "divine/human relations" in the early Barth, but before *CD* II/2 he did not "push" actualism "back" into God's being.[11]

The second major change in Barth, according to McCormick, came with his use of terminology in later writings. McCormack believes Barth's actualized theological ontology is connected with his change in terminology.

> After the change, Barth began to develop the outlines of a more thoroughly actualistic ontology which supplanted the traditional categories of "person," "natures," Godhead, and so on… It is well known that the later Barth eliminates the classical distinction of loci on the "person" and "work" of Christ, that he integrates the "two natures" doctrine with that of the "two states," and that he uses the "threefold office" of Christ to order the material which would classically have been treated under the headings "divine nature," "human nature," and the "unity" of the two, respectively.[12]

In sum, the major changes from the earlier to the later Barth, according to McCormack, are in the areas of (1) actualistic theological ontology more consistently applied, and (2) terminology being used to replace the traditional terminology.

THE CHALCEDONIAN CREED

Regarding Chalcedon, McCormack believes Barth has a better solution to the theological problems the fathers faced.[13] According to McCormack, the wording of the creed

---

[11] Ibid., 202, 213.
[12] Ibid.
[13] Ibid., 203-6.

of Chalcedon was more in keeping with the theology of Cyril of Alexandria. McCormack quotes from this section of the creed: "one and the same Christ, Son, Lord, only-begotten, to be acknowledged in two natures, inconfusedly, unchangeably, indivisibly, inseparably; the distinction of natures being by no means taken away by the union, but rather the property of each nature being preserved, and concurring in one Person and one Subsistence." The proposition that two natures are unified in the one Person is meant to deny that Christ is two persons (Nestorianism).[14] The affirmation of the one Person, Christ, who is the foundation or ground for the two natures is that which is "decisive" in the creed.[15] This subject is identified as the Word. McCormack believes the union of the two natures is an improper way of explaining the incarnation because of a possible misunderstanding, and so he gives this clarification:

> I should add that the language employed here was ill-suited to the purposes of the writers in one respect. The council did not really intend to speak of a union of two "natures" as its language suggests; it was not the divine "nature" which was incarnated but the Logos, the Second Person of the Trinity. So what is brought together is actually, in the strictest sense, the Logos and a human "nature."[16]

Furthermore, the term "human nature" is unclear in its meaning in the creed and has two possible senses: (1) general or universal, in which "manhood" is a proper translation, or (2) individual, where it refers to "a man."[17]

---

[14] Nestorianism is described as affirming two persons in Christ (5th century heresy).

[15] Ibid., 203-4.

[16] Ibid.

[17] Ibid.

The first is preferred because it guards against adoptionism and also points to Christ's redemption as universal in scope.[18]

McCormack believes two major problems were never solved by the creed. The first is the *communicatio idiomatum*, and the second problem is the identification of the "subject" who did the work of redemption.[19] The fathers would have said the "Logos *simpliciter*—that is, two natures in one person (identified as the Logos)."[20] It is in this second "issue" where more problems come in if certain "values" are not upheld.[21] "Logically, the basic idea that the divine Word is hypostatically united with a full and complete human nature could also suggest that the subject is the God-human in his divine-human unity but this answer could be consistently maintained only where two values were protected."[22] What are these two "values" that must be protected in order to maintain a unity of the "God-human"? The first value is to guard "the full and free cooperation of the human element in the work of the divine." The second value is to avoid "dissolving the unity of the person."[23]

---

[18] Adoptionism teaches that the human Jesus became God's Son at his baptism and received special powers from God at that time. It rejects that Jesus is the eternal Son of God.

[19] The *communicatio idiomatum* (communication of properties) refers to the communication of proper attributes from Christ's divine and human nature to his one person. Where the Reformed and Lutheran differ on the communication of properties, see Richard A. Muller, *Dictionary of Latin and Greek Theological Terms: Drawn Principally from Protestant Scholastic Theology* (Grand Rapids: Baker Academic, 1995), 72-74.

[20] Ibid., 205.

[21] Ibid.

[22] Ibid.

[23] Ibid.

For the Chalcedonian fathers to keep these two values would be very difficult because of two other problems or "obstacles." The first problem was Cyril of Alexandria's notion of making the divine dominant over the human nature in the Logos. This violates the first theological value that the human nature must be free and not bound or directed by the divine nature.[24] The second "obstacle was the abstract metaphysical understanding of divine immutability presupposed. For most, it was unthinkable that God should suffer and die. Suffering and death entail 'change' and God cannot change. So there was a perceived need to assign suffering and death to the human 'nature' alone." [25] With a Greek metaphysical understanding of God's being, which is static and self-contained, the Chalcedonian fathers were really unable to solve the problem of God's immutability—they were inconsistent. Barth saw this problem and spent most of his life resolving it with his actualistic theological ontology, which consistently maintains the theological values laid out above. "The red thread that runs through the whole of Barth's theology—and that gives to his theological ontology its character as relational and actualistic—is the strictly theological problem of the meaning of divine immutability in relation to the fact of the incarnation."[26] The problem with God's immutability not being compromised when God becomes incarnate is seen in the question, "How is it possible for God to 'become' human without undergoing

---

[24] Ibid.

[25] Ibid.

[26] Bruce McCormack, "The Being of Holy Scripture Is in Becoming: Karl Barth in Conversation with American Evangelical Criticism," in *Evangelicals & Scripture: Tradition, Authority and Hermeneutics*, ed. Vincent Bacote, Laura C. Miguelez, and Dennis L. Okholm (Downers Grove, IL: Inter Varsity Press, 2004), 74.

some kind of profoundly ontological change?"[27] Barth seeks to solve the problem by actualizing the eternal being of God and not holding to a Greek metaphysical "substance," which he saw as compromising the goodness of God and the deity of Christ, both of which are affirmed in the confession, "The Lord is Jesus."[28] "It was for this reason that he [Barth] felt compelled to actualize the doctrine of the incarnation. He turned to post-Kantian philosophies in order to help him explicate what he understood to be a genuinely theological state-of-affairs."[29]

The line of demarcation is thus clear between Barth and the Chalcedonian fathers. They operated with a different view of God's being (theological ontology), and this is the major difference between them. Barth saw the early church forming its doctrines of election, the Trinity, and Christ out of a commitment to abstract Greek philosophy, and he believed modern post-Kantian philosophy was better at developing and explaining these doctrines.[30]

It is at this point that Barth sees the Chalcedonian fathers and the Reformed orthodox *not* holding to a unity of the person of Christ because they assign suffering and death to the human nature alone. The charge is that they are leaning toward a Nestorian view of Christ and cannot truly hold to the deity of Christ.[31] Barth sees the Reformed as

---

[27] Ibid.

[28] Ibid., 74-75.

[29] Ibid., 75.

[30] Ibid.

[31] Ibid., 74-75. McCormack says of Barth, "His concern is with the coherence of our confession that the Lord is Jesus. His basic conviction, from very early on, was that the early church's commitment to the Greek philosophical category of 'substance' must finally undermine the coherence of its confession of the deity of Christ." For the Nestorian charge, see *Orthodox and Modern*, 206.

separating ("abstracting") the natures when they assign the death of Christ to his human nature only. The fathers were properly motivated in wanting to maintain God's immutability, but to assign Christ's death to his human nature alone is "deeply problematic." [32] The unity of the Person of Christ has been compromised ("surrendered"). [33] In pointing to one nature of Christ with regard to any activity, the fathers have made that nature a "subject," so that one has to affirm two subjects. [34] They have also made the human nature the "object" of the divine subject, which takes away the freedom of the human in relation to the divine nature. [35] As we will see in Barth's christological progression, this problem is solved with an actualized theological ontology. [36]

What is the "source" of this problem the fathers had when they attributed an activity such as death to the human nature of Christ and moved in a Nestorian direction? McCormack answers,

> Their source is a process of thought which "abstracts" the Logos from his human "nature" in order, by turns, now to make the human "nature" something to be acted upon by the Logos and now to make of that "nature" a subject in its own right in order to seal the Logos off hermetically from human experiences such as death. In both cases, the Logos has been "abstracted" from the human "nature" and

---

[32] McCormack, *Orthodox and Modern*, 205.

[33] Ibid., 206.

[34] Ibid.

[35] Ibid., 205.

[36] This sentence is my opinion and observation after reading McCormack. He repeatedly has mentioned Barth's different theological ontology, which is actualized, as the difference Barth has with the orthodox, but he also sees it as a necessary correction to have coherence in theology.

made into an abstract metaphysical subject (the Logos *simpliciter*).[37]

Clearly, Barth's solution is "in the rejection of the abstract metaphysical subject of Chalcedon and in its replacement with an understanding of the Redeemer as a subject whose reality is constituted by a twofold history (the humiliation of God and the exaltation of the human)." Here McCormack's Barth has replaced Christ's two natures with the new term "history." So, according to McCormack, Barth developed "a new and different theological ontology (of the divine, of the human, and of the God-human)."[38] This is clearly seen in his mature doctrine on reconciliation (*CD* IV/1-3) which comes after his reworking of the doctrine of election (*CD* II/2). We will now look at the development of Barth's Christology.

THE EARLY CHRISTOLOGY OF BARTH IN *CHURCH DOGMATICS* I/2

McCormack transitions to his second major section, "Church Dogmatics I/2, Section 15." Here he begins to show the historical progression of Barth's Christology from his early writing of *CD* I/2 to the doctrine of election in *CD* II/2, and then his mature doctrine of Christ in *CD* IV/1-3. It is in this first attempt at the doctrine of Christ (*CD* I/2) that there is continuity and discontinuity with regard to Barth's later writings. For instance, in *CD* I/2 he treats a special Christology but rejects such a category in *CD* IV/1-3. The mature Barth of *CD* IV/1 rhetorically questions: "But where do we find a special Christology?—A Christ in Himself, abstracted from what He is amongst the men of

---

[37] McCormack, *Orthodox and Modern*, 206.
[38] Ibid.

Israel and His disciples and the world, from What He is on their behalf? Does He ever exist except in this relationship?"[39] The later Barth clearly sees no *Logos asarkos* ("without flesh") and attempts a more consistent theological ontology where "the being of Jesus Christ…is his work." [40] The later Barth did not have a special Christology where the Person and Work of Christ were distinguished. However, the early Barth did have a special Christology because he surprisingly (in *CD* I/2 section 15) had, at times, an abstract Greek metaphysical ontology underlying his theological ontology. "Granted, this lapse into metaphysical thinking is exceptional in Barth's theology even at this time."[41] So, in the early Barth we could say he is more in line with the Chalcedonian fathers. He uses the terminology of "person" and "natures" which he later replaces with the term "history."[42]

Another significant difference with the early Barth is found in an effort to maintain God's immutability where again his rare slip into Greek metaphysical thinking shows through. McCormack quotes Barth, "God's 'Word would still be his Word apart from this becoming, just as Father, Son and Holy Spirit would be none the less eternal God, if no world had been created.'" [43] McCormack interprets, "What this affirmation would seem to imply is that the being of the Word is something complete in itself without respect to the 'becoming' which he would undergo in entering time. And the problem which this understanding poses very directly is that of *how* the Word could then

---

[39] Ibid., 206-7.
[40] Ibid., 207.
[41] Ibid.
[42] Ibid. 208.
[43] Ibid., 209.

'become' without undergoing change?"[44] Barth would later answer the problem of divine immutability with an actualistic theological ontology. This early Barth sees the divine Word having a different ontology than the human nature.[45] The later Barth because of his actualistic ontology sees the change in the human nature affecting the divine Word. But the early Barth can say "the Word assumed flesh" in reference to the "becoming" in John 1:14. For the Barth of *CD* I/2 "'movement' or 'change' is located on the level of existence, where it can have no significance for that which the divine Word is."[46] The later Barth would assign movement or change to the eternal being of God by way of the concrete event of Jesus Christ in election, where Jesus is both the subject and object of election. This later move by Barth would eliminate his violation of God's immutability in *CD* I/2 section 15. And because of the evidence of Greek metaphysical ontology, as shown above, it is more accurate to say that the early Barth is Chalcedonian in his Christology.

---

[44] Ibid. McCormack in a similar manner says, "It is here that Barth slips most visibly into the substantialist form of ancient metaphysics where his Christology is concerned. What is common to substantialist forms of ancient metaphysics as applied to the problem of an ontology of the person is the thought that what a person 'is' is something that is complete in and for itself, apart from and prior to all the decisions, acts, and relations that make up the sum total of the lived existence of the person in question" (211).

[45] Ibid., 212.

[46] Ibid., 211.

BARTH'S REVISION OF ELECTION

McCormack's third section is "Christology in the Light of Election (*CD* II/2)." It is in the doctrine of election[47] where major changes occur and Barth's actualism is more consistently applied "and pushed back into the eternal being of God."[48] With Barth's change in the doctrine of election there is a major change in theological ontology where God's eternal being is constituted by his eternal decision to be for us (*pro nobis*). "This is not a decision for mere role-play; it is a decision with ontological significance. It is a free act in which God assigned to himself the being God would have for all eternity."[49] How is this revision of election related to God's eternal being? One of its results is "that it makes

---

[47] For a more complete study on Barth's doctrine of election, see "Grace and Being: The Role of God's Gracious Election in Karl Barth's Theological Ontology," in McCormack, *Orthodox and Modern*, 183-200. McCormack's essay "Grace and Being" sparked a controversy among Barthians. For another Barthian view on the relationship between the Trinity and election, see George Hunsinger, "Election and the Trinity: Twenty-five Theses on the Theology of Karl Barth," in *Trinity and Election in Contemporary Theology*, ed. Michael T. Dempsey (Grand Rapids: Eerdmans Publishing Company, 2011), 91-114. McCormack has a response to Hunsinger in the same volume entitled, "Election and the Trinity: Theses in Response to George Hunsinger," 115-37. McCormack admits to having gone beyond Barth on this matter of the Trinity being a function of election ("Grace and Being," 192). McCormack uses Barth as a resource because he believes he is the best, and he believes to just quote him and not draw out the implications of his theology is a misuse of Barth. He sees Barth as a means to an end and not an end in himself ("Election and the Trinity: Theses in Response to George Hunsinger," 137).

[48] McCormack, *Orthodox and Modern*, 213. McCormack states, "At this stage [*CD* I/2] of his development, actualism is certainly present in all of Barth's descriptions of the divine-human relation established in revelation. But it has not yet been pushed back into the eternal being of God."

[49] Ibid., 216.

God so much the Lord that he is even the Lord over his own 'essence.' For this reason, Barth would later assert that God is not by accident a suffering God but is so 'essentially.'"[50] Also, Christ is not just the *object* of election, he is also its *subject*. For Barth this change in the subject of election determined the nature of election and is the most "revolutionary" part in his revision of election. [51] McCormack explains, "To make Jesus Christ the subject of election—if carried out consistently—is to bid farewell to the distinction between the eternal Word and the incarnate Word."[52] Now Barth would say there is no Word who is complete in and of himself from the Word who assumed flesh in time. The immanent Trinity and the economic Trinity are the same in content; there is no distinction.[53] God's will is primary and is the basis (or ground) for his eternal being. This results in an answer to the problem of divine immutability in relation to the incarnation, because there is now no change in God's eternal being by the incarnation, because God has eternally decided his essence based upon his decision ("self-determination" and "self-limitation") to become flesh in time.[54] The eternal being of God is Jesus Christ. The second person of the Trinity *is Jesus Christ essentially* and not the *Logos asarkos*. There is no eternal Son of God without flesh. However, the Logos does

---

[50] Ibid.

[51] Ibid.

[52] Ibid., 217.

[53] Ibid.

[54] In historicizing the doctrine of Christ, McCormack teaches that God is essentially humble and obedient because the being of God is constituted by Jesus' eternal decision to redeem all humanity. See Bruce L. McCormack, "Divine Impassibility or Simply Divine Constancy? Implications of Karl Barth's Later Christology for Debates over Impassibility," in *Divine Impassibility and the Mystery of Human Suffering*, ed. James F. Keating and Thomas Joseph White, O.P. (Grand Rapids: William B. Eerdmans Pub., 2009), 185.

not have literal flesh from all eternity but does have it eternally by way of anticipation. In this way, it can be said, the essence of God is Jesus Christ. When the incarnation is actualized by way of Jesus Christ being both the subject and object of election, the doctrine of immutability is redefined and that "value" (of immutability) is preserved. For Barth, divine immutability is a "constancy" in God's being which is Jesus Christ from all eternity.[55] The Chalcedonian fathers' definition of immutability was violated by the incarnation because the Logos who was incarnated was an abstract metaphysical Person. For the fathers change occurred at the level of existence only.

BARTH'S MATURE CHRISTOLOGY

It is in McCormack's last section, "The Christology of the Doctrine of Reconciliation," where the mature doctrine of Barth's Christology shows through. This is *CD* IV:1-3. The previous section on election (and specifically that Jesus Christ is the subject who elects) makes clear that there is no *Logos asarkos* in Barth's theology—certainly not the way the Chalcedonian fathers saw it (i.e. the Logos complete in and of Himself). "So there is no 'eternal Son' if by that is meant a mode of being in God which is not 'identical with Jesus Christ.' Therefore Jesus Christ is the electing God."[56] Why no *Logos asarkos*? Because "the second 'Person' of the Godhead in Himself and as such is not God the Reconciler." [57] Barth's radical reworking of election is consistently carried forward into his Christology and forms its basis. "The root of Barth's Christology is to be found in

---

[55] Ibid., 177.
[56] McCormack, *Orthodox and Modern*, 219.
[57] Ibid.

his doctrine of election." [58] Barth's actualized theological ontology is consistently applied to his doctrine of election and Christology so that there can be no *Logos asarkos*. "If God is who and what God is in the act in which God is 'with us,' then we may not abstract from this act to seek a being of God above and behind this act."[59] Barth now has a satisfactory answer to the problem of divine immutability which the fathers could not give because of their abstract theological ontology. [60] However, Barth's new actualized theological ontology has a new problem which is "that of reflecting upon the unity of a Subject whose being is constituted both in time and in eternity by a two fold history."[61]

It is here, with Barth's mature Christology as seen in his doctrine of "reconciliation," where two key terms of Chalcedon are replaced. "Nature" is replaced by "history"

---

[58] Ibid., 223.

[59] Ibid.

[60] For a clear understanding of how Barth's actualized ontology better explains the problems of God's impassibility and immutability, see Bruce L. McCormack, "The Actuality of God: Karl Barth in Conversation with Open Theism," in *Engaging the Doctrine of God: Contemporary Protestant Perspectives*, ed. Bruce L. McCormack (Grand Rapids: Baker Academic, 2008), 219-23. McCormack states, "If the Logos is the Subject of the human sufferings of Jesus, then suffering is an event which takes place *within the divine life*—which also means that the divine 'nature' cannot be rightly defined in abstraction from this event. The divine nature can rightly be defined only by this event. The net consequence of this move is that *Barth is able to advance an understanding of divine immutability which is no longer controlled by the further thought of impassibility.* If becoming human, suffering and dying, and so forth, are the content of the eternal decision in which God gives himself his being, then no change is introduced into the being of God when this becoming and so forth take place in time. And if God is immutably determined for suffering, then the concept of immutability has been cut loose from impassibility" (pp. 222-23) (emphasis original).

[61] McCormack, *Orthodox and Modern*, 222.

and "history" is "integrated" into "Person." Even with this change in terminology there is a formal similarity with Barth's new doctrine of Christ and Chalcedon in that he can still affirm Christ's "'true divinity'" and "'true humanity.'" Therefore, the difference between the two (Barth and Chalcedon) is *material* because of his actualized ontology.[62] So Barth can affirm the *true divinity* and the *true humanity* of Christ, but in name only, not in the *substance* of those terms, as in Chalcedon.[63]

It cannot be overemphasized, as noted above, that Barth's Christology is only properly understood in the context of his doctrine of election, with its actualized ontology. For instance, Barth's revised doctrine of election explains God's self-humiliation which is difficult to understand. McCormack elucidates, "God's 'true being' is seen in his death on the cross bearing sin." [64] In the incarnation there is no paradox because we learn what God *is* by the incarnation and the work of Christ. For Barth the being of God is not an unknown which is what it is when there is a *Logos asarkos*. God's ontology (essence) is determined by what he decides to be for us. The "true" nature of God is seen in Jesus' death on the cross.[65]

Furthermore, the mature theology of Barth still holds to a distinction between the *anhypostasia* and *enhypostasia* with reference to the "human Jesus" (showing it "has no independent existence"), but now the theological ontology is different; it is not Greek metaphysical essence, but it is "actualized," meaning the will is *primary* and determines

---

[62] Ibid.

[63] Ibid. See n52 where McCormack takes George Hunsinger to task for his stance that Barth's Christology is "basically" Chalcedonian. McCormack sees this characterization as "misleading."

[64] Ibid., 225.

[65] Ibid.

God's essence as realized in time in the economy of salvation. God chooses what his being will be and this is an eternal choice.[66] McCormack clarifies, "No longer is it a question of subsistence in an abstract metaphysical subject. Here it is a question of living from the gracious decision of election." Also, with an actualized theological ontology there is no "divinization" of the human Jesus but there is *participation* of the divine being in the human being and vice versa, but this participation is "asymmetrical." Both divine being and human being are constituted in Jesus Christ in the one "primal decision" of election.[67]

For the mature Barth there are *not* two "natures" in Christ but now two "histories." How does Barth achieve the unity of the "Person" of Christ with this change in terminology? The answer is found in election where "the unity of what might seem to be two distinct histories finds its ground in the 'primal decision' of God in election."[68] God's essence for Barth is "concretely realized." [69] Jesus Christ is "the God-human...not only in time but already in eternity."[70] As McCormack said earlier, Jesus Christ is the name of the second person of the Trinity.[71]

CONCLUSION

To sum up McCormack's interpretation of Barth, the major difference between Barth and Chalcedon is in their theological ontology. Barth's is actualized, theirs is not, and this is the material difference Barth has from Chalcedon.

---

[66] Ibid., 226.
[67] Ibid., 223, 226-28.
[68] Ibid., 228.
[69] Ibid.
[70] Ibid., 229.
[71] Ibid., 223-24.

The theological ontology the Chalcedonian fathers presupposed was *static, complete,* and *immutable* in itself, without any reference to God's relationship with his creation or the incarnation. In form, the early Barth was the same as Chalcedon, but with his mature theology came a formal change as well. The terms "person" and "natures" were replaced by the term "history." With Barth's major revision of election came a redefining of divine immutability as well. There was no change in God's being with the incarnation because God's being was eternally determined to be Jesus Christ. The existence of Jesus Christ in the economy of salvation had ontological consequences to God's eternal essence. In other words, existence determined essence. So God's very nature was humble and obedient from all eternity because of his *decision* to be God *for us* in Jesus Christ.

Barth is both orthodox and modern, according to McCormack. His modernity is reflected in his actualized theological ontology[72] which means he is anti-metaphysical. Though he has made major corrections to Chalcedon, he is still orthodox because he retained its "theological values."[73] Having heard from McCormack, the Charles Hodge Professor of Systematic Theology, we now turn to his nineteenth-century predecessor, Charles Hodge himself, to explore his Christology and to compare it with McCormack's Barth.

---

[72] Ibid., 232. See n76 for a full explanation of modernity as it relates to Barth.

[73] Ibid., 229. Also see McCormack, "Actuality of God," 221. McCormack makes it clear that the actualized ontology of Barth makes it possible to keep the "theological values" found in Chalcedon. He lists three values of Chalcedon as (1) one person Christology, (2) Jesus' "full divinity" and (3) "full humanity" upheld (221).

CHAPTER 2

THE CHRISTOLOGY OF CHARLES HODGE: OLD PRINCETON SPEAKS

To help us establish what the church has traditionally taught about Christology, we will be looking at the Chalcedonian Christology of Charles Hodge (1797-1878), the third professor of Princeton Seminary. Our aim in this and the following chapter is to define what Chalcedonian Christology has been for the Christian church, and to then compare and contrast it with the modern proposal of Bruce McCormack. In the end we will see a radically different Christology than the fathers confessed. Chapters 2 and 3 compare Old and New Princeton Christologies.

It is important to note that Hodge was a confessing Christian and minister in the Presbyterian Church in America his entire adult life, and he believed that faith was grounded in the Scriptures and faithfully articulated in the Westminster Confession of Faith. He also expressed on several occasions during his long career at Princeton Seminary that no new doctrine ever came from that

institution.[74] It may be debated whether that was completely
true, but the motivation and intent of the man was to
faithfully teach the truth of Scripture, as articulated by the
Westminster Standards, to the culture in which he lived.[75]
While Scottish Common Sense Realism did influence his
language and is evidenced throughout his writings, it is my
contention that Common Sense Realism was not driving his
theological commitments.[76]

---

[74] See A. A. Hodge, *The Life of Charles Hodge* (Edinburgh: Banner of
Truth Trust, 2010), 275, 460. Charles Hodge specifically wrote
concerning the articles in the *Princeton Review*, of which he was the
editor, that "they [the authors] have advanced no new theories, and
have never aimed at originality. Whether it be a ground of reproach or
of approbation, it is believed to be true that an original idea in
theology is not to be found in the pages of the *Biblical Repertory and
Princeton Review* from the beginning until now" (275). In a personal
correspondence to Dr. Cunningham, Hodge gives a glimpse into what
was driving his theological writing; he says: "I have had but one
object in my professional career and as a writer, and that is to state
and to vindicate the doctrines of the Reformed Church. I have never
advanced a new idea, and have never aimed to improve on the
doctrine of our fathers. Having become satisfied that the system of
doctrines taught in the symbols of the Reformed Churches is taught
in the Bible, I have endeavoured to sustain it and am willing to believe
even where I cannot understand" (460). For more recent biographies
on Charles Hodge, see W. Andrew Hoffecker, *Charles Hodge: The Pride
of Princeton* (Phillipsburg, NJ: P&R Publishing, 2011); Paul C. Gutjahr,
Charles Hodge: Guardian of American Orthodoxy (New York: Oxford
University Press, 2011).
[75] See James J. Cassidy, "No 'Absolute Impeccability': Charles Hodge
and the Christology at Old and New Princeton," *The Confessional
Presbyterian* 9 (2013):143-56. Cassidy demonstrates that Hodge did go
beyond the received tradition (19th century) with his view that Christ's
human nature in itself was not absolutely impeccable, and was more
faithful to Chalcedon's view of Christ being truly man than his
contemporaries.
[76] For a good understanding of Scottish Common Sense Realism, see
Mark Noll, *America's God: From Jonathan Edwards to Abraham Lincoln*
(Oxford: Oxford University Press, 2002), 93-113. Noll explains that
Common Sense Realism "was, first, a localized example of the 'new
moral philosophy' of the seventeenth and eighteenth centuries, whose

proponents set aside Aristotelian and scholastic Christian authorities in search for what they considered better axioms upon which to base theories of human nature, psychology, and morality. In the words of Norman Fiering, the premiere student of the subject, 'The guiding assumption behind almost all of the new work was the belief that God's intentions for man, His expectations of human beings as moral creatures, could be discovered independently of the traditional sources of religious authority, through a close investigation of human nature.' Generically considered this new moral philosophy promoted 'commonsense moral reasoning,' or an approach to ethics self-consciously grounded upon universal human instincts" (94). For more on Common Sense Realism, see K. Scott Oliphint, *Reasons for Faith: Philosophy in the Service of Theology* (Phillipsburg: P&R Publishing, 2006), 141-42. For a fuller understanding of the debates concerning Scottish Common Sense Realism in the old Princeton theology, see Paul Kjoss Helseth, *"Right Reason" and the Princeton Mind: An Unorthodox Proposal* (Phillipsburg, NJ: P&R Publishing, 2010). Helseth gives an alternate yet plausible interpretation of the place of reason and faith at Old Princeton. He sets forth a thesis that the "right reason" for the Princetonians was not "intellectual" but "moral" and assumed and even stated that this reason was a regenerated reason and that the whole person and not just the intellect was being appealed to by the Princetonians. His "unorthodox" proposal is a well-researched challenge to the notion that the Princetonians viewed "right reason" as autonomous and "speculative," which would be how secular philosophy views it. Helseth supports the view that the epistemology of the Princetonians was consistent with their Reformed theology and heritage. Also see Mark A. Noll, ed., *The Princeton Theology 1812-1921: Scripture, Science, and Theological Method from Archibald Alexander to Benjamin Warfield* (Grand Rapids: Baker Academic, 2001), 107; and David B. Calhoun, *Princeton Seminary*, vol. 2, *The Majestic Testimony, 1869-1929* (Edinburgh: The Banner of Truth Trust, 1996), 414. Calhoun aptly says, "The Princetonians never allowed Scottish Common Sense Philosophy to stand by itself or to determine their theological outlook. Far more important than their philosophical views were their biblical and confessional commitments. They made their philosophy serve their theology not the other way around" (414).

AN "ANTHROPOLOGICAL ANALOGY"[77] AND SCRIPTURAL FOUNDATION OF THE HYPOSTATIC UNION

Hodge begins his discussion on the person of Christ with a preliminary look at the human makeup, which serves as a key analogy for his Chalcedonian formulation that Christ is one person with two distinct natures—divine and human.[78] Hodge states that every human is one person with two aspects: (1) a material body and (2) an immaterial soul, and that these two aspects though distinct are unified in each person.[79] Christ also is one person with a dual nature, and this is not impossible or contradictory because in our own realm of experience, with the human makeup, we see an illustration of the same concept.[80] Hodge next states that "the nature of the union between the soul and body" is the following: (1) "A personal union," (2) "a union without mixture or confusion" and (3) "not a mere inhabitation, [or]

---

[77] See Cassidy, "No 'Absolute Impeccability,'" 147, where he uses the term "anthropological analogy."

[78] Why did Hodge defend orthodox Christology so firmly and consistently? There were a number of factors and influences in his life. I see four prominent ones: (1) Archibald Alexander's influence, (2) his high view of Scripture, (3) his commitment to the Westminster Standards, and (4) his commitment to Reformation tradition (Augustine, Calvin, Turretin, Edwards, et al.).

[79] This human makeup analogy goes back, at least, to the Athanasian Creed, paragraph 37, which states: "For as the reasonable soul and flesh is one man: so God and Man is one Christ" found in Philip Schaff, *The Creeds of Christendom: With a History and Critical Notes*, 6th ed. (Grand Rapids: Baker Books, 2007), 2:69. Francis Turretin also used the analogy, although Hodge used it more; see Francis Turretin, *Institutes of Elenctic Theology*, trans. George Musgrave Giger, ed. James T. Dennison, Jr. (Phillipsburg, NJ: P&R Publishing, 1994), 2:321.

[80] Charles Hodge, *Systematic Theology* (Grand Rapids: Wm. B. Eerdmans Publishing Co., 1995), 2:378-80.

a union of contact or in space." [81] This three-fold description of personal union reflects the language and meaning of the Chalcedonian creed. First, under "personal union," Hodge is stressing the fact that a human being is *one* person who experiences life from what the mind and body does (not a dual personality). Second, in stating that the union is "without mixture or confusion," he is stressing that the two aspects of body and soul retain their peculiar properties and *do not mix* and convert into a third thing (*tertium quid*). Two elements converting to a third thing is illustrated in brass which is made of the combination of copper and zinc. [82] Third, this personal union of two elements is not an indwelling, such as a person living in a house or being in one's clothes. [83] This structure of one person comprised of two aspects is *key* to Hodge, and it is upon this structure that he fleshes out his Christology.

As the human analogy illustrates the nature of the union between two elements, it also shows five "consequences." The first is called the "communion of attributes" and means that "the person is the possessor of all the attributes, both of the soul and the body."[84] Though each aspect of man (body and soul) has attributes that are unique to it, Hodge sees it as crucial to understand that it is the person who possesses these attributes. As he explains, "Whatever is true of either element of his constitution is true of the man…each [aspect of man] has its properties and changes, but the person or man is the subject of them all." [85] The second consequence makes the point that "apparently contradictory" things may be said of the person

---

[81] Ibid., 2:378-79.

[82] Ibid., 2:378.

[83] Ibid., 2:379.

[84] Ibid.

[85] Ibid.

because each aspect of the person has different qualities and each of these qualities is true of the one person. Hodge gives an example: "We may say that he is weak and that he is strong; that he is mortal and immortal; that he is a spirit, and that he is dust and ashes."[86] The third consequence has reference to the fact that a person may be named by one of his aspects, say a quality of the body, and have as the "predicate" the quality of the other aspect, the soul. Hodge explains, "We call him a spirit and yet say that he hungers and thirsts. We may call him a worm of the dust [the body is in view] when we speak of him as the subject of regeneration [something that happens to the soul]."[87] The fourth consequence refers to actions of the body or the soul as being the actions of the person. So, Hodge is logically taking his above points about the attributes and now making the same point with reference to human activity. Hodge explains, "It is the man who thinks; it is the man who speaks and writes; and the man who digests and assimilates his food."[88] It is the one person who is acting according to either aspect (body or soul). His fifth and final consequence is that "this hypostatic union is the exaltation of the body."[89] So the personal union of every person's body and soul gives the body an "exalted" status. Hodge elucidates further that "the reason why the body of a man and its life are so immeasurably exalted above those of a brute is that it is in personal union with a rational and immortal soul. It is this also which gives the body its dignity and beauty."[90] Hodge's point is that man is higher than the

---

[86] Ibid.
[87] Ibid.
[88] Ibid.
[89] Ibid.
[90] Ibid., 2:379-80.

rest of creation because of his "intellectual beauty." [91] Hodge illustrates, "The mind irradiates [brightens or illuminates] the body, and imparts to it a dignity and value which no configuration of mere matter could possess." Both mind and body will be united in the glorified state of man in the new heavens and the new earth.[92] What Hodge is clearly saying by all of this, is that man's basic constitution of one person with two aspects is an illustration pointing to the person of Christ having a union of two natures, divine and human. It is not a perfect illustration at every point but it is adequate. Furthermore, just as there is mystery in the operations of a human's two elements, so there is mystery in Christ's two natures in one person. Hodge sees great apologetic value in this analogy: "There is in this case enough of resemblance to sustain faith and rebuke unbelief." He is convinced that what he has said about man's constitution is clearly seen though it is denied by some, and he is equally convinced that what the Bible teaches about Christ's person is clear.[93]

We turn now to where Hodge gets his support for his Chalcedonian Christology—the Scriptures. Hodge saw the exposition of Scripture as the source for his theology and *not* philosophical speculation. A. A. Hodge, in describing the transition of his father from professor of the ancient languages to systematic theology, made the point that his father was engaged in biblical exegesis during the first twenty years, and that this was great preparation for his new position in systematic theology.[94] Dr. William Paxton in

---

[91] Ibid., 2:380.

[92] Ibid.

[93] Ibid.

[94] A. A. Hodge, *The Life of Charles Hodge*, 342. A. A. Hodge states: "Thus, in a way in which for him [Charles Hodge] it was alone possible, he was led to make acquisitions in the original languages of

describing his former teacher of theology said about Hodge's method and attitude toward Scripture,

> With him, the simple question was. What do the Scriptures teach? And when this was ascertained by the light which the study of the original languages and exegetical investigation threw upon it, he did not think that it was our province to stop and inquire whether this was in harmony with our own reason, but to accept it with an humble and trustful spirit. When God speaks, and we understand its meaning, there is nothing left for us but to bow and adore.[95]

Having seen Hodge's high regard for Scripture in formulating doctrine, we turn to look at his exegetical and systematic skill in developing his doctrine of Christ's person. He saw Scripture teaching three major points about Christ's person: (1) Christ has a "complete" human nature (truly man), (2) Christ has a "perfect" divine nature (truly God), and (3) Christ is one person. That Christ is truly a man means that Christ had a "complete human nature" (body and soul) like any other person, except for sin. Second, that Christ is truly God means that "everything that can be predicated of God can be predicated of Christ." Third, that Christ is one person means "the same person, self, or Ego, who said, 'I thirst,' also said, 'Before Abraham was, I am.'" And Hodge sees these three statements about Christ's person as "the whole doctrine of the incarnation as it lies in the Scriptures and in the faith of the Church."[96] The ancient symbols of Nicene and Chalcedon are seen in

---

Scripture and in the science and practice of Biblical exegesis, which are professedly the basis of systematic theology, and yet are the qualification in which the vast majority of speculative theologians have been more or less deficient."

[95] Ibid., 629.

[96] Hodge, *Systematic Theology*, 2:380.

these three points. Hodge says, "The proof of this doctrine includes three distinct classes of passages of Scripture, or may be presented in three different forms." The first class or form of scriptural proof (also called "arguments") looks at the three major points about Christ's person and defines in more detail what each concept entails and gives scriptural proof.[97] Hodge calls these three points "facts." The first *fact* is that Christ is "truly man" and Hodge stresses that Christ's body was *real* (not docetic), in every way like all humans except for sin, and that this body came from his earthly mother and *not* from heaven:

> He had a true body and a rational soul. By a true body is meant a material body, composed of flesh and blood, in everything essential like the bodies of ordinary men. It was not a phantasm, or mere semblance of a body. Nor was it fashioned out of any heavenly or ethereal substance. This is plain because he was born of a woman.[98]

Scriptures that point to this fact are Hebrews 2:14 and Luke 24:39. In explaining what the rational soul meant he gave no specific scriptural texts but specifically said it is seen in the fact that Christ "thought, reasoned, and felt; was joyful and sorrowful; He increased in wisdom; He was ignorant of the time when the day of judgment should come. He must, therefore, have had a finite human intelligence." What makes Christ a complete man? That he has a real human body and a rational soul.[99] Each of these *facts* is found in the Gospels. The second *fact* about Christ's person is he is truly God. Jesus has the names, titles, and attributes (omnipresent, omniscient, omnipotent,

---

[97] Ibid.
[98] Ibid., 2:381.
[99] Ibid.

immutable) of God, and performs divine activities (creator, sustainer and ruler of the world) that alone are God's and ascribed to him. He is called God and is worshipped which is only right of God. Hodge emphatically exclaims that "God is not more, and cannot promise more, or do more than Christ is said to be, to promise, and to do."[100] The third *fact* about Christ's person is that he is *one* person. Negatively proved, there is no evidence in Scripture of Christ being two persons. There are distinct persons in the Trinity but not in Christ's person. The positive proof in Scripture is found in how Christ is addressed, always as singular *you*, and how he refers to himself, "I, me, mine." In other words, Christ is never referred to in the plural but always with a *singular* pronoun.[101]

The second form of scriptural passages teach that Christ is at the same time man and God. In the Old Testament, Christ is said to be a man when he is from the tribe of Judah and a son of David. He is also called Immanuel and the Mighty God, etc., which points to his divine nature. In the New Testament Christ is represented in both ways as well. Jesus calls himself a man, as do his disciples. He also calls himself the Son of God and is called God by the Apostles. The importance and seriousness of this doctrine is declared by Hodge when he notes, "These conflicting representations, this constant setting forth the same person as man, and also as God, admits of no solution but in the doctrine of the incarnation. *This is the key to the whole Bible. If this doctrine be denied all is confusion and contradiction.*"[102] What is the great mystery of godliness? The answer according to Hodge is, "Christ is both God and man, in two distinct natures, and one person forever." The

---

[100] Ibid., 2:382.
[101] Ibid., 2:383.
[102] Ibid., 2:383-84 (emphasis mine).

uniqueness of the incarnation is captured when Hodge declares that "God manifest in the flesh is the *distinguishing doctrine of the religion of the Bible, without which it is a cold and lifeless corpse.*"[103] Hodge is saying that without the incarnation there is no genuine Christianity, so to distort this doctrine in any way is detrimental to the teaching and life of the church. This is why he is painstakingly laying out the particulars of the incarnation by way of Chalcedon: (1) Christ is truly God, (2) Christ is truly man, and (3) Christ is one divine person. To deny the distinctness of the two natures which adhere in the one person of Christ is non-Christianity.

THE *LOGOS ASARKOS* IN JOHN 1:1-14, ROMANS 1:2-5, AND PHILIPPIANS 2:6-11

The third form for the proof of Christ's person is an examination of some specific passages. Hodge makes clear that this doctrine is taught in all of Scripture and is not taught by proof-texting. Hodge treats six christological texts—John 1:1-14; 1 John 1:1-3; Romans 1:2-5; 1 Timothy 3:16; Philippians 2:6-11; Hebrews 2:14—and in each of these he sees the three main facts of Chalcedon taught about the Logos (truly man, truly God, one person). Though Hodge does not use the term *Logos asarkos* (Word without flesh) he believes in the eternal Son. In John 1:1-14 he lists ten different things about the Logos taken from the text. We will mention some of those points pertinent to our discussion. This passage teaches that the Logos was eternal and in an intimate relationship with God (vv. 1-2). The Logos was God (v. 1). The Logos was the Creator of all things (vv. 3, 10). The Logos had life and light in himself

---

[103] Ibid., 2:384 (emphasis mine).

(vv. 4-5). The Logos assumed human nature in time (v. 14). Hodge highlights the main points of this passage in his summary of John 1:14:

> It is here taught that a truly divine person, the eternal Word, the Creator of the world, became man, dwelt among men, and revealed himself to those who had eyes to see, as the eternal Son of God. Here is the whole doctrine of the incarnation, taught in the most explicit terms.[104]

Another important point he makes about John 1:1-14 in his Romans commentary is that the Logos (λόγος) is also the Son (υἱός) in v. 18 who is "in the bosom of the Father."[105]

In Hodge's Romans commentary under Romans 1:3 he explains at length what the term Son means in the New Testament. It is "not a term of office" but a word which indicates he is the second person of the Trinity and coessential with the Father. In looking at the word "Logos" (λόγος), Hodge sees two ways it is used in Scripture. The first usage is the Logos referred to as our Creator, and the second usage is the Logos enfleshed (the historical God-man). In Hebrews 1:2 Hodge believes the Logos is used in both ways: "has spoken to us by his Son" refers to the incarnated Logos and "whom [his Son] he appointed the heir of all things, through whom also he created the world"

---

[104] Ibid. The two natures Christology of Chalcedon is a fundamental for Hodge, as seen in his comment on 1 John 1:1-3: "The incarnation is declared to be the characteristic and essential doctrine of the gospel." Ibid., 2:384-85.

[105] Charles Hodge, *A Commentary on Romans* (1864; repr., Edinburgh: Banner of Truth Trust, 1997),18. Recent Greek texts which were not available to Hodge have a better attested reading of John 1:18, which is μονογενὴς θεὸς (the only God) instead of ὁ μονογενὴς υἱός (the only begotten Son). This newer reading is a stronger attestation to Christ's deity.

refers to the Logos without flesh.[106] In Romans 1:3-4 both usages of Logos are seen. In verse 3 the enfleshed Logos is in view: "concerning his Son, who was descended from David according to the flesh" (v. 3). Verse 4, "And was declared to be the Son of God in power according to the Spirit of holiness by the resurrection from the dead, Jesus Christ our Lord," has reference to the *Logos asarkos*, the Logos who was our Creator.[107] Concerning the word "Son" Hodge says that it

> designates the divine nature of Christ. In all cases, however, it is a designation implying participation of the divine nature. Christ is called the Son of God because he is consubstantial with the Father, and therefore equal to him in power and glory. The term expresses the relation of the second to the first person in the Trinity, as it exists from eternity…He was and is the Eternal Son….Christ was not predestinated to be the Son of God. He was such from eternity.[108]

Contemporary Reformed exegesis agrees with Hodge's meaning of the Son. Where there is disagreement with his exegesis is his defining "according to the Spirit of holiness" (κατὰ πνεῦμα ἁγιωσύνης) to refer to the divine nature.[109] In

---

[106] All Scripture quotations are from the English Standard Version unless noted otherwise.

[107] Charles Hodge, *Romans*, 17, 18.

[108] Ibid., 18, 19.

[109] Recent Reformed scholars such as John Murray interpret the phrase "according to the Spirit of holiness" to be not a reference to Christ's divine nature but to a new era in redemptive history. See John Murray, *The Epistle to the Romans: The English Text with Introduction, Exposition, and Notes* (Grand Rapids: Eerdmans, 1997), 10-12; Richard B. Gaffin Jr., *Resurrection and Redemption: A Study in Paul's Soteriology*, 2nd ed. (Phillipsburg, NJ: P&R Publishing, 1978), 98-113. For a detailed exposition of the Logos in John 1:1-14, see Geerhardus Vos, *Redemptive History and Biblical Interpretation: The Shorter Writings of*

his Romans commentary Hodge gives other strong proofs that the term Son refers to the deity of the second person of the Trinity. He goes to passages in John's Gospel and the Epistles where Jesus is called the Son of God, is equal to the Father in authority, power, glory, and essence, and does the works of God, such as creation (cf. John 5:17-31; 10:29-42; Col. 1:13-17). In Hebrews 1:4-6 the Son is superior to the angels and is entitled to be worshipped. All this proves that the Son and the Logos are the same and they are God.[110]

Hodge considers Philippians 2:6-11 to be the most "full and explicit" passage on the incarnation. It teaches that the same person in the "form of God" (v. 6) in time assumes the "form of a servant" (v. 7) without ceasing to be in the "form of God." The "form of God" (μορφῇ θεοῦ) means Christ is essentially equal to the Father, and the "form of a servant" (μορφὴν δούλου) means Christ is like a man (consubstantial) in every way, except for sin. Hodge is careful the word "form" is not misunderstood. He gives the definition of the term and explains how it is uniquely applied to the eternal Son by Paul. He states that "nature" is implied by the word μορφη: "The form of a thing is the mode in which it reveals itself: and that is determined by its nature. It is not necessary to assume that μορφη has here, as it appears to have in some other cases, the sense of φύσις; the latter is implied in the former. No one can appear, or exist in view of others in the form of God, i.e., manifesting

---

Geerhardus Vos, ed. Richard B. Gaffin Jr. (Phillipsburg, NJ: P&R Publishing, 2001), 59-90. For an explanation of the Logos as he relates to epistemology, see K. Scott Oliphint, "Bavinck's Realism, The Logos Principle, and Sola Scriptura," *Westminster Theological Journal* 72 (2010): 359-90.
[110] Hodge, *Romans*, 18.

all divine perfections, who is not God."[111] Jesus in "the form of God" has the full divine nature.[112]

ADDITIONAL EXEGESIS IN SUPPORT OF HODGE ON PHILIPPIANS 2:6-11

As a brief excursus from Hodge, but in the spirit of Hodge's Old Princeton exegesis, we will look at the exegetical work of Lane G. Tipton in an essay entitled, "The Presence of Divine Persons: Extending the Incarnational Analogy to Impeccability and Inerrancy."[113] Tipton echoes Hodge's exegesis on Philippians 2:6-11 as he underscores the primacy of the divine and the subordination of the human in the incarnation. Hodge believes the eternal Son remains in the form of God after the incarnation, and Tipton's exegesis concurs. We will first look at the Christ hymn and the three main "theological categories" found in Philippians 2:6-11:

    A.   Preexistence: v. 6

        1.   ὃς ἐν μορφῇ θεοῦ ὑπάρχων
        2.   οὐχ ἁρπαγμὸν ἡγήσατο τὸ εἶναι ἴσα θεῷ,

---

[111] Hodge, *Systematic Theology*, 2:385-86.

[112] Hodge defines φύσις (nature) as "the source or origin of any thing in the character or condition, it always expresses what is natural or innate, as opposed to what is made, taught, superinduced, or in any way incidental or acquired." Charles Hodge, *Ephesians* (1856; repr., Edinburgh: Banner of Truth Trust, 1991), 68.

[113] Lane G. Tipton, "The Presence of Divine Persons: Extending the Incarnational Analogy to Impeccability and Inerrancy," *The Confessional Presbyterian* 6 (2010): 200.

B.   Incarnation: vv. 7-8

1.   ἀλλὰ ἑαυτὸν ἐκένωσεν
2.   μορφὴν δούλου λαβών,
3.   ἐν ὁμοιώματι ἀνθρώπων γενόμενος·
4.   καὶ σχήματι εὑρεθεὶς ὡς ἄνθρωπος
5.   ἐταπείνωσεν ἑαυτὸν
6.   γενόμενος ὑπήκοος μέχρι θανάτου, θανάτου δὲ σταυροῦ.

C.   Exaltation: vv. 9-11

1.   διὸ καὶ ὁ θεὸς αὐτὸν ὑπερύψωσεν
2.   καὶ ἐχαρίσατο αὐτῷ τὸ ὄνομα τὸ ὑπὲρ πᾶν ὄνομα,
3.   ἵνα ἐν τῷ ὀνόματι Ἰησοῦ πᾶν γόνυ κάμψῃ ἐπουρανίων καὶ ἐπιγείων καὶ καταχθονίων
4.   καὶ πᾶσα γλῶσσα ἐξομολογήσηται ὅτι κύριος Ἰησοῦς Χριστὸς εἰς δόξαν θεοῦ πατρός.[114]

Tipton makes helpful points from this text which strengthen Hodge's exegesis. The first is establishing that the basic theological categories of (1) preexistence, (2) incarnation, and (3) exaltation are typical of Paul. Their order is significant and logical ("eternal preexistence" precedes incarnation in time and then exaltation). Second, the preexistent Christ who is in "the form of God" remains in that form of equality with God after taking on the form of a servant. Tipton shows how the present active participle (ὑπάρχων) indicates that "the form of God" is not being lost by the "addition" of "the form of a servant" (i.e. taking

___

[114] See ibid.

on flesh). Third, the preexistence of the Son, "the form of God" (μορφῇ θεου), provides the context in which the incarnation is able to take place. And lastly, the exaltation is the reward for the Son taking on "the form of the servant" and dying for the sins of his people (vv. 7, 8). Tipton stresses that the "emptying himself" (ἑαυτὸν ἐκένωσεν) is explained by the taking (λαβών aorist active participle) of "the form of the servant" (μορφὴν δούλου) vv. 7, 8. There is no "subtraction" in the incarnation, only an "addition."[115]

Having laid the groundwork of how a human being serves as an *analogy* for the person of Christ, and how the Bible plainly teaches that Christ is one person with two natures (human and divine) which remain *distinct* and *unmixed*, Hodge next treats two things which the church has taught and *must continue* to teach about Christ's person: (1) the *nature* of this hypostatic union and (2) the *consequences* of this hypostatic union.[116]

THE NATURE OF THE HYPOSTATIC UNION

In light of errors taught about Christ's person, the church has made the *nature* of the hypostatic union clear. There is a real union of the divine and human natures in the one person of Christ. At the outset, what is most crucial to this discussion of the hypostatic union is the term "substance."[117] For Hodge, to give up the language and concept of *substance* is against Scripture and what was generally accepted in the history of human thought; therefore, the concept of substance is "necessary." Giving it up is not an option. Where there are activities or attributes

---

[115] Ibid.
[116] Hodge, *Systematic Theology*, 2:387.
[117] Ibid.

present there is a substance or subject underneath them. Negatively put, he says, "Of nothing, nothing can be predicated."[118] So important is this concept of substance, it bears repeating four "principles" that are "self evident" according to Hodge. In this context it is important to remember that substance and nature are used synonymously and point to how he views the nature of the hypostatic union. His four principles about substances are the following: (1) any evidence of an attribute or an activity implies a substance, (2) attributes are consistent with what the substance is and are unique to it (e.g. the finite cannot become infinite and vice versa), (3) attributes and substances are inseparable, and (4) substances cannot transfer their attributes to another substance. These four principles are what comprise the nature of this hypostatic union of two natures.[119] There is an overlap with these four principles but it shows how important they are to Hodge as he applies them to the person of Christ. His initial point is that two substances (natures) are united in the one person of Christ and that these two natures are real, complete, and adhere in Christ, so that He is truly man in every sense of that term, except for sin, and that He is truly God with all attributes unique to God. The union of the two natures in Christ does not obliterate the two natures so that the human always remains creaturely and the divine always

---

[118] Ibid.

[119] Substance is a philosophical term, but Hodge used the form and not the content of philosophy, according to Helseth. Helseth is convinced that "the religious epistemology of the Princeton theologians was principally informed by anthropological and epistemological assumptions that are consistently Reformed." He does not deny any Scottish Common Sense Realism influence but he does not see it as great or primary an influence as have others such as Sydney Ahlstrom. See Helseth, *"Right Reason" and the Princeton Mind*, xxv (emphasis mine).

remains God. It is *impossible* for these natures to cease to be what they are. Hodge's first point about the nature of the hypostatic union is that it a union of two distinct natures *which remain distinct.*[120]

Second, the nature of this hypostatic union does not involve a mixing or blending of the two into a third thing (*tertium quid*) so that the natures are lost. Hodge makes a fine distinction about the term God-man that needs noting because some see the union of the two natures resulting in a "theanthropic" nature (a third thing). His distinction is that "Christ's person is theanthropic, but not his nature; for that would make the finite infinite, and the infinite finite. Christ would be neither God nor man; but the Scriptures constantly declare Him to be both God and man."[121] Also, under this second point, Hodge makes it clear that Christ has two wills because both natures have the qualities of intelligence and will.[122] He gives clarity to this concept when he says, "His human intellect increased, his divine intelligence was, and is infinite."[123]

The third point about a hypostatic union of natures in Christ is that the human nature cannot transfer attributes to the divine nature or vice versa. If this could happen then both natures would cease to be what they are and therefore would lose their identity.[124] The fourth point is that the union of the two natures in Christ is *personal,* meaning a divine person is united with a complete human nature. It is in this final point where Hodge makes it clear that the personality of Christ is one, and that this personality resides in his divine person and not the human nature. The human

---

[120] Hodge, *Systematic Theology*, 2:388.

[121] Ibid., 2:389.

[122] Ibid., 2:389-90.

[123] Ibid., 2:390.

[124] Ibid.

nature of Christ was and is impersonal in itself. A crucial point made is that "it was a divine person, not merely a divine nature, that assumed humanity, or became incarnate. Hence it follows that the human nature of Christ, separately considered, is impersonal."[125] That Christ's human nature is impersonal in itself has traditionally been called *anhypostatic* and *enhypostatic* Christology, though Hodge does not use this terminology.[126]

THE CONSEQUENCES OF THE HYPOSTATIC UNION

The consequences of Christ's hypostatic union of natures are seen first in a "communion of attributes" (*communicatio idiomatum*) and second in Christ's *actions*. In other words, a real personal union of the human and divine natures in Christ's one person entails no communication of properties between the natures. This keeps the natures *distinct* and yet in a *real inseparable* union. Hodge, in keeping with the received tradition, believes the attributes of each nature are communicated *only* to the person. Christ's one person operates out of both natures (communication of operations).[127] The attributes of the human nature cannot be transferred to the divine nature and vice versa. For Hodge, that is an impossibility. [128] Hodge finds the communion of attributes to the one person of Christ in

---

[125] Ibid., 2:391.

[126] *Enhypostatic* means that Christ's human nature derives its personality from its union with the divine person of the Logos. *Anhypostatic* means that the human nature by itself has no personality.

[127] Hodge does not use the term *communicatio operationum* (communication of operations) but he is describing it here. It has reference to Christ's one person acting out of both natures. See Muller, *Dictionary of Latin and Greek Theological Terms*, 74-75.

[128] Hodge, *Systematic Theology*, 2:392.

four types of passages. The first, and most common, is where Christ is named not in reference to one of his natures but in reference to both natures, names such as "our Redeemer, our Lord, our King, Prophet, or Priest, our Shepherd." Other examples are when Christ is described as "our wisdom, righteousness, sanctification, and redemption." [129] The second group of passages is where what is predicated of the one person of Christ is attributable to his divine nature only, which is the eternal Logos.[130] The third group of passages predicates of Christ's person an attribute from his human nature only. [131] The fourth category is where the one subject of Christ is named from his divine nature but what is predicated of him is true of both natures. [132] In Hebrews 1:1-3 Hodge sees Christ referred to with flesh (God-man) in one instance (v. 2), and without flesh (eternal Son) as the Creator (v. 3), and as the God-man with reference to his human nature when he died for our sins (v. 3b).[133]

The second consequence of the hypostatic union of Christ's human and divine natures is similar to the first consequence but looks at the activities of Christ. Sometimes Christ is named as to his divine nature but does an act that is human only, such as eating or drinking. Other times

---

[129] Ibid.

[130] An example given is in John 8:58, "Before Abraham was I am." Ibid.

[131] Examples are Christ being sorrowful, thirsty, hungry, tired, and ignorant of the time of judgment (Mark 13:32). Ibid., 2:393.

[132] He references 1 Cor. 15:28 where the Son will be subject to the Father and explains that it is the God-man in view and not just one of his natures. Another passage is where Jesus says "the Father is greater than I" (John 14:28b). He explains that "The Father is not greater than the Son, for they are the same in substance and equal in power and glory. It is as God-man that He is economically subject to the Father." Ibid., 2:393-94.

[133] Ibid., 2:394.

Scripture shows Christ being named as to his human nature and acting according to his divine nature, such as forgiving sins.[134] Hodge ends this section with concluding proofs of Christ being the God-man, such as he was able to receive worship which a man cannot rightly receive, and came to be a savior able to sympathize with us which God or man alone cannot do. Concerning sympathizing, Hodge explains that

> He is just the Saviour we need. God as God, the eternal Logos, could neither be nor do what our necessities demand. Much less could any mere man, however wise, holy, or benevolent, meet the wants of our souls. It is only a Saviour who is both God and man in two distinct natures and one person forever, who is all we need and all we can desire.[135]

Having given a brief outline of Hodge's Christology we now will turn to see how he and McCormack compare. In comparing the old and new Princeton Christologies we will see there have been significant changes.

---

[134] Ibid., 2:395.
[135] Ibid., 2:396.

CHAPTER 3

NEW VERSUS OLD PRINCETON: MCCORMACK CONTRASTED WITH HODGE

Where Hodge ends his treatise on Christ's person, we will begin our comparison of the two Princeton professors. Hodge concludes by giving a concise summary of Chalcedonian Christology:

> The simple, sublime, and saving Christology of the Bible and the Church universal is: "That the eternal Son of God became man by taking to Himself a true body and a reasonable soul, and so was and continues to be God and man in two distinct natures and one person forever.[136]

Hodge's views lead to a contrast with McCormack's Christology in these four areas: (1) attitudes toward the creeds and confessions of the church, (2) views of the distinction between Christ's two natures, (3) views of the Creator/creature distinction, and (4) attitudes toward philosophy.

---

[136] Ibid., 2:454.

ATTITUDES TOWARD THE CREEDS AND CONFESSIONS OF THE CHURCH

Hodge's first point in critiquing the modern Christologies of his day was that they were in opposition to what the universal church had believed for the past eighteen hundred years in the creeds and confessions. He saw modern Christology as "a departure from the faith of the Church,"[137] primarily, a departure from Chalcedon (A.D. 451) and also from the sixth ecumenical council at Constantinople (A.D. 681). Specifically in reference to a Reformed Christology, Hodge quotes from the Second Helvetic Confession, chapter 11, and the Westminster Confession of Faith 8.2. [138] He saw these symbols as accurate expressions of what the Bible taught and what Christians believed about Christ's person. Hodge further believed that the Bible *alone* was the sole authority for the believer's faith and practice and that these symbols were authoritative as they were faithful expressions of Scripture's teaching. While McCormack and Barth profess to value these creeds, they do not seem to see them as authoritative in the way that Hodge saw them.[139] McCormack believes Barth viewed the creeds as a "human witness" with a relative binding authority.[140] In connection with this, it is important to note that Barth did not see the Bible as *directly*

---

[137] Ibid., 2:437.

[138] Ibid., 2:404-7.

[139] McCormack stresses that Barth valued the creeds but his confessionalism was "of the spirit" and not "the letter" of the creed's wording; see McCormack, *Orthodox and Modern*, 17. For Hodge's attitude on creedalism, see "What is Meant by Adopting the Westminster Confession?," in A. A. Hodge, *The Westminster Confession: A Commentary* (1869; repr., Edinburgh: Banner of Truth Trust, 1998), 420-26.

[140] McCormack, *Orthodox and Modern*, 232-33.

revealing God's will, but only as a witness to revelation, and not revelation itself. For Barth, revelation was Jesus Christ and *indirect*.[141] This is a huge epistemological contrast with a Reformed epistemology which views God's revelation as *directly* received by its recipients. [142] McCormack explains Barth's attitude toward the Chalcedonian creed and all creeds:

> Karl Barth never held the Chalcedonian dogma to be anything more than a human witness to a subject matter which he too was seeking to express. As the decree of an ecumenical council, it was granted a relatively binding human witness, a witness that exceeded that of other witnesses, but a witness all the same. And a witness is not the thing itself. This is why Barth was able to be so free in his appropriation of its insights and values. This is why his encounter with Chalcedon was not finished in a moment but consisted in a history characterized by growth and change. Here as elsewhere, it is important to remember what Barth said with respect to the dogmas of the church: *"Dogmas are not veritates a Deo formaliter revelatae*. In dogmas it is the Church of the past that speaks. This is venerable. It deserves respect. It is normative. It speaks *non sine Deo*, as is fitting. Yet it is still the Church. In dogmas the Church defines, i.e., limits revealed truth, the Word of God. The Word of God thus becomes the word of man. It is not an insignificant word. Indeed, it is a supremely significant word. Yet it is still the word of

---

[141] For Barth's view on revelation being indirect see, McCormack, *Orthodox and Modern*, 81-84, 110-12, 153, 214, 282.

[142] For a Reformed epistemology, see Cornelius Van Til, *An Introduction to Systematic Theology: Prolegomena and the Doctrines of Revelation, Scripture, and God*, ed. William Edgar (Phillipsburg, NJ: Presbyterian and Reformed, 2007), chs. 3-5; also K. Scott Oliphint, *Reasons for Faith: Philosophy in the Service of Theology* (Phillipsburg, NJ: Presbyterian and Reformed, 2006), chs. 5-8.

man. The Word of God is above all dogmas as the heavens are above the earth."[143]

We can appreciate with Barth that Chalcedon, like all creeds, are products of the church and so, from men. We would add they are *not* infallible or inerrant as Scripture is. However, we do see Chalcedon as the church setting forth what the Scriptures teach concerning Christ's person. Hodge was convinced that the creeds are expressions of what the Bible clearly taught:

> If the Bible be the only infallible rule of faith and practice; and if the Bible be a plain book, and if the Spirit guides the people of God (not the external church, or body of mere professing Christians) into the knowledge of the truth, then the presumption is invincible that what all true Christians believe to be the sense of Scripture is its sense.[144]

Hodge saw Chalcedon as an expression of what the universal church believed was "the obvious sense of Scripture." [145] It seems Barth and McCormack view Chalcedon as a "human witness" that may have gotten it wrong. To them it is *not* an accurate expression of what God has revealed in his inerrant Word, the Bible. Since Scripture, the norm of all norms, is not a direct, accessible revelation from God, we do not have anything fixed or certain on Barthian soil. The creed for McCormack is not an expression of a fixed truth found in an inerrant revelation.

---

[143] McCormack, *Orthodox and Modern*, 232-33 (the English italics are McCormack's).
[144] Hodge, *Systematic Theology*, 2:437.
[145] Ibid., 2:427.

Chalcedon and the So-called Unattended Issues

McCormack sees Chalcedon as leaving two issues unsettled and therefore *open to interpretation*: (1) the communication of properties between the natures, and (2) the identity of the one person. He says this about Chalcedon and these supposed unsettled matters:

> Notwithstanding this great achievement, the Chalcedonian formula did leave at least two very significant Christological issues *unattended* that continue to haunt theology in both West and East right up through the present day. This is not surprising since these issues were not controverted at the time. But the *open-endedness* of the formula where these issues are concerned did have the effect of leaving the formula itself *exposed to interpretations* that would continue to lead the churches into error.[146]

Did Chalcedon leave the communication of properties (*communicatio idiomatum*) and the identity of Christ's one person "unattended" as McCormack asserts? Not so according to Hodge:

> The Reformed Church in adhering to the doctrine as it had been settled in the Council of Chalcedon, maintained that there is such an *essential* difference between the divine and the human natures that the *one could not become the other, and that the one was not capable of receiving the attributes of the other.* If God became the subject of the limitations of humanity He would cease to be God; and if man received the attributes of God he would cease to be man. This was regarded as a self-evident truth. The "communion of attributes" which the Reformed, in accordance with the common faith of the Church, admitted,

---

[146] McCormack, "The Ontological Presuppositions of Barth's Doctrine of the Atonement," 350-51 (emphasis mine).

concerned only the *person* and *not* the natures of Christ. Christ possessed all the attributes of humanity and of divinity, but the two natures remained *distinct*; just as a man is the subject of all that can be predicated of his body and his soul, although the attributes of the one are not predicable of the other.[147]

Hodge believes Chalcedon is clear about the natures not being able to transfer or receive attributes from each other. They are "sealed off" so to speak, and kept *distinct* but not separated or mixed. Chalcedon did not leave this issue unattended as McCormack asserts, and the Reformed clearly articulated Chalcedon on the two natures in the Westminster Confession of Faith when it described them as "whole, perfect, and distinct natures, the Godhead and the manhood…inseparably joined together in one person, without conversion, composition, or confusion. Which person is very God, and very man, yet one Christ, the only Mediator between God and man."[148] It should be further noted that Hodge was repeating the Reformed tradition when he said the attributes of each nature were communicated to the person and not nature to nature. This is a biblical communication of properties.[149]

---

[147] Hodge, *Systematic Theology*, 2:409 (emphasis mine).

[148] WCF 8.2.

[149] Hodge observed that the Lutheran position was a departure from the universal church's position on the communication of properties. He states that the Lutheran position on the communication of attributes was "peculiar to that church and forms no part of Catholic Christianity"; see Hodge, *Systematic Theology*, 2:418. Hodge's exposition and critique of Lutheran Christology is found in 2:407-18.

Chalcedon and the Term *Substance*

When Hodge chided modern Christology for rejecting the creed of Chalcedon, he pointed to the clear, accepted language of *consubstantial* which was universally understood. As we have seen, McCormack rejects the concept of *substance*. Hodge sees the rejection of *consubstantial* as a fundamental error. It is not just a difference in the formal wording of the creed, but a radical change in the *meaning* of the term substance (nature). The verbal *form* may be the same with McCormack at times, but the *meaning* or *content* of that form is completely different. This was no small matter of interpretation over secondary issues for Hodge, as he makes clear:

> There is no dispute as to the sense in which the Council used the word *nature,* because it has an established meaning in theology, and because it is explained by the use of the Latin word consubstantial, and the Greek word ὁμοούσιος. Nor is it questioned that the decisions of that Council have been accepted by the whole Church.[150]

McCormack agrees to the meaning of the term substance and its cognates. Why he abandons it will be made clearer as we look at the hypostatic union of the two natures and finally God's being itself as it relates to immutability.[151]

---

[150] Ibid.

[151] For McCormack's understanding of substance in Greek thought, see McCormack, *Orthodox and Modern,* 211; and McCormack, "The Ontological Presuppositions of Barth's Doctrine of the Atonement," 356-57.

VIEWS ON THE DISTINCTION OF CHRIST'S TWO NATURES

Hodge is zealous to preserve the *integrity, reality,* and *wholeness* of the two natures in Christ's person and to keep them *distinct.* He sees Chalcedon as stating that both natures are *equally necessary* if God chooses to redeem a people for himself (which he did). If the Redeemer does not have a complete divine and complete human nature then we do not have a Savior whom we can worship nor one who can sympathize with our weaknesses, and finally make a permanent, infinite, and efficacious atonement for our sins. Hodge writes, "It is only a Saviour who is both God and man in two distinct natures and one person forever, who is all we need and all we can desire....We are therefore complete in Him, wanting nothing."[152] As we saw above, McCormack rejects the concept of substance or nature, which Hodge stated was "necessary" in having an orthodox view of Christ's person.[153] Without the concept of *substance* it is impossible to keep the two natures distinct. The distinction of the two natures is foundational to maintaining a robust Chalcedonian Christology. Hodge states, "The idea of substance is a necessary one." Consequently, to reject the idea of a "substance" ends the conversation for Hodge.[154] It

---

[152] Hodge, *Systematic Theology,* 2:396. Hodge in stressing the necessity that our redeemer be both infinite God and finite man in one person says, "It is to this fact [the incarnation] that the infinite merit and efficiency of his work [of redemption] are due" (2:396).

[153] Ibid., 2:387.

[154] See Hodge, *Systematic Theology,* 2:387. Hodge states that when opponents deny the four principles about substance which he has set forth then "their denial puts an end to discussion."

is here that the two professors would be at an impasse.[155] McCormack makes the two natures "history," as well as the one person.[156] In this modern move, there is not a two natures Christology, but rather one eternal nature which is the God-human, Jesus Christ. It is interesting to note that, according to Hodge, a preexistence of Christ's humanity was seen in Swedenborg (1688-1772), a Swedish theologian, and it was found in another modern Christology which proclaimed, "The incarnation of God is from eternity."[157] McCormack also sees the incarnation of Christ as eternal. In gleaning from Dorner's work on Christology, Hodge makes some observations which are in line with the Christology of McCormack:

> We have the authority of Dorner for saying that the modern speculations on Christology are founded on the two principles that there is but one nature in Christ, and that human nature is *capax naturae divinae*, is capable of being made divine. To this must be added a third, although Dorner himself does not hold it, that *the divine is capable of becoming human*.[158]

McCormack's Christ does not have two distinct natures, truly divine and truly human. There are two histories instead of two natures, but this does not comport with the Bible as defined at Chalcedon. The chief principle of modern Christologies is a rejection of two distinct natures for one nature instead. This one nature of

---

[155] Jim Cassidy explains, "Here, in Hodge's understanding of nature, we find the foundation for a proper distinction of the two elements of the hypostatic union." Cassidy, "No 'Absolute Impeccability,'" 149.

[156] McCormack, *Orthodox and Modern*, 228-29.

[157] Hodge, *Systematic Theology*, 2:429 (emphasis original).

[158] Ibid., 2:430 (emphasis mine).

McCormack's Christ is divine-human (Jesus Christ) from all eternity.[159]

The second principle about modern Christology Hodge gleaned from Dorner had to do with a transfer of attributes (*communicatio idiomatum*) from the divine nature to the human nature. This the Lutherans did, but Hodge logically saw a third possibility, which Dorner did not make, and that is a transfer of attributes from the human nature to the divine. McCormack sees Chalcedon as "open" on this issue and believes in a transfer of properties from the human nature to the divine (Logos). He states that "we would do well to revise the Chalcedonian formula just a bit so that the elaboration of an 'abstract' doctrine of the Logos as the redeeming subject is rendered impossible." His chart shows the communication of properties in one direction from the human nature to the Logos only, with an oval around it and the one subject on top.[160] Hodge on the other hand offers no major corrections to Chalcedon like this. For him, the identity of the person of Christ is the eternal Son of God, the second person of the Trinity who is the *Logos asarkos* (without flesh) before time, and the *Logos ensarkos* (with flesh) at the time of the incarnation. McCormack would call this an abstraction which Hodge would deny. His conviction, based on Scripture, was that "It was the Logos [*asarkos*] which became man; and not a God-man that assumed a material body." [161] One of the serious consequences of this rejection of the Logos without flesh

---

[159] McCormack says, "In this view [Barth's making the person and natures history], the Reconciling Subject is no longer the Logos *simpliciter* (the abstract metaphysical subject) but the God-human in his divine-human unity. And he is this not only in time but already in eternity." McCormack, *Orthodox and Modern*, 229.

[160] McCormack, "The Ontological Presuppositions of Barth's Doctrine of the Atonement," 355.

[161] Hodge, *Systematic Theology*, 2:427.

and this new interpretation which transfers the human nature to the Logos is that the divine is lost and humanized. With no proper distinction of natures and a communication of properties between them which results in one nature, as in the case of McCormack, the result is a god who is human which is not the God of the Bible. Hodge would see this in principle as Eutychian, but it is an eternal Eutychianism.[162] Hodge in expositing Dorner on modern Christology and the two natures said this: "Any *distinction of natures*, in the ordinary sense of the words, must, he [Dorner] says, be given up. It is on this assumption that the modern views of the person of Christ are founded."[163] Sadly, it is a characteristic of modern Christologies that they eschew all distinctions in theology (e.g. person and work of Christ).[164] McCormack's Christology certainly fits this description because he has given up the normal way the word *nature* is used and refuses to distinguish the *divine* from the *human*. We will now turn to something closely related to this discussion of two distinct natures—the Creator/creature distinction.

VIEWS ON THE CREATOR/CREATURE DISTINCTION

McCormack states that Barth has a Creator/creature distinction, just as he professes a "two natures" Christology.[165] Modern Christologies violate the classic metaphysical distinction between the divine and the human

---

[162] Ibid., 2:438.

[163] Ibid., 2:428 (emphasis mine).

[164] Ibid., 2:433.

[165] For the assertion of Barth's Creator/creature distinction by McCormack, see McCormack, *Orthodox and Modern*, 191, and for his affirmation of a two natures Christology, see ibid., 16.

which classical theology sees as a *qualitative* difference between God and creation. Though the Creator/creature terminology is not used by Hodge, he believes in the concept but uses different terminology. For instance he calls it a "proper dualism between God and the world, and between God and man." [166] Hodge evaluated different forms of modern Christology, and that of Schleiermacher in particular drew this insight which is worthy of meditation. It gets to the essence of the problem with modern Christologies:

> Theologians of this class deny that God and man are essentially different. They repeat, almost with every breath, that God and man are one, and they make this the fundamental idea of Christianity, and especially of Christology. [167]

Though this insight is pre-Barth (by 40 years at least!), it reveals a major flaw in the modern Christological scheme and why it cannot be considered Christian in the historic/biblical sense of the word. It makes God and man identical, and this is one of the chief errors. The whole edifice is built on a so-called "actualistic" theological ontology which is a view of God's essence that is humanized and historicized (as we saw above). Hodge saw this identification of God and man as that which their whole theology and Christology are based on. Looked at rationally (and positively), when there is no essential difference between God and his creation, many of the problems of theology are solved, or so it seems, such as immutability in relation to the incarnation. McCormack says the Logos without flesh (*Logos asarkos*) when he became incarnate, as the Chalcedonian fathers taught, really violated

---

[166] Hodge, *Systematic Theology*, 2:444.
[167] Ibid., 2:429.

God's immutability (unchangeableness). McCormack believes an absolute Logos who then takes on flesh involves an essential change in God. [168] This is not true of the orthodox position, but this is how it is portrayed and essentially charged with not being orthodox. The orthodox/Reformed position admits there is great mystery in the incarnation, but not an essential change in the second person of the Trinity. A. A. Hodge, Charles Hodge's son, gives clear help here with what change occurs at the incarnation of the eternal Son. To the question, "What were the effects of this personal union upon the Divine nature of Christ?" the following answer is given by A. A. Hodge:

> His divine *nature* being eternal and immutable, and, of course, incapable of *addition*, remained *essentially unchanged* by this union. The whole immutable divine essence continued to subsist as the eternal Personal Word, now embracing a perfect human nature in the unity of his person, and as the organ of his will. Yet thereby is the *relation* of the divine nature changed to the whole creation, since he has become Emmanuel, "God with us," "God manifest in the flesh."[169]

There is no essential change in the eternal Son at the time of the incarnation, only a change in relationship with the creation. Both Hodges assert no essential change in the second person of the Trinity at the time of incarnation. The Logos remains *a se* ("of himself" and independent) while *contingently* taking on a real human nature in time. Hodge's

---

[168] McCormack, "The Ontological Presuppositions of Barth's Doctrine of the Atonement," 356-57.
[169] A. A. Hodge, *Outlines of Theology* (1860; repr.,Edinburgh: Banner of Truth Trust, 1999), 382 (emphasis mine).

Reformed commitments refuse to go beyond the Scripture to explain the mystery of this union of two natures.[170]

ATTITUDES TOWARD PHILOSOPHY

So far we have seen differences in confessionalism, in views of the hypostatic union itself—the communion of properties and the identity of the person—and in understanding the Creator/creature distinction. Now we come to a different attitude toward philosophy.

Both men, Hodge and McCormack, have a tremendous grasp and appreciation for philosophy. Both claim to eschew speculation and abstraction in theology, and each would profess their theology is in line with Chalcedon and Scripture. But as we have seen up to this point there is a vast difference between these two schools of thought.

It would be helpful to reflect on McCormack's explanation of the role philosophy plays in the theology of Barth. It has an authoritative role and not one of service, as the Reformed have viewed it. McCormack, in explaining the orthodoxy of Barth's theology, asks a question of philosophy's role and seeks to show how Barth is modern in his theological/philosophical commitments and still orthodox:

> And most important, perhaps, is it necessary to affirm the philosophical commitments which aided the ancients and the Reformers in their efforts to articulate the theological subject matters under

---

[170] A. A. Hodge explains the cognitive limits concerning the personal union of two natures in Christ. He states, "Yet it does not become us to attempt to explain the manner in which the two spirits mutually affect each other, or how far they meet in one consciousness, nor how the two wills co-operate in one activity, in the union of the one person." Ibid., 380.

consideration? Or may one draw upon more modern philosophies in one's effort to explain the creeds and confessions today? My own view is this: what Barth was doing, in the end, was seeking to understand what it means to be orthodox under *the conditions of modernity*. This is the explanation, I think, for the freedom he exhibited over against the decrees of the ecumenical councils and the confessions of his own Reformed tradition. He took the creeds and confessions seriously—how could he not, believing as he did in the virgin birth and so forth? But he did not follow them slavishly. His was a confessionalism of the spirit and never of the letter. This is why he was willing to think for long stretches with the help of Kant's epistemology and the (later) Hegelian ontology. This is why he was willing to set forth an actualistic understanding of divine and human being. Still, I would argue, his reconstruction of Christian orthodoxy succeeded in upholding all of the theological values that were in play in its originating formulations. For this reason, Barth was both modern *and orthodox*.[171]

It seems McCormack believes the ancient church was committed to a philosophy in doing its theologizing. I believe this assumption is wrong. Philosophy did *not* have a magisterial or constitutive role.[172] Briefly put, Scripture was

---

[171] McCormack, *Orthodox and Modern*, 16-17 (emphasis original).

[172] For an excellent resource for understanding philosophy's role in ancient creedal formulation of the 4th century see R. P. C. Hanson, *The Search for the Christian Doctrine of God: The Arian Controversy, 318-381* (Edinburgh: T&T Clark, 1988). His treatment of philosophy's role can be found throughout the book, but a section from the introduction is a good start. In the introduction Hanson tells what part it played or did not play in the discovery of the doctrine of God. He writes, "The subjects under discussion between 318 and 381 were not, as has sometimes been alleged, those raised by Greek theology or philosophy and such as could only have been raised by people thinking in Greek terms. It was not simply a quarrel about Greek ideas. ...It was the problem of how to reconcile two factors which

the norm of norms and philosophy had a secondary role with its use of language and concepts. Even with the philosophical concepts that were used, a formal similarity but biblical meaning was poured into those terms. In sum, philosophy was serving in the creedal formulations but it was not the *principia* (foundation or source). Also, the "values" McCormack has in mind are the two natures in one person formula, but the content or meaning of *nature* and *person* is actualized, which is contrary to the Chalcedonian fathers. He admits all this but believes he and Barth have the liberty to change the meaning of natures and

---

were part of the very fabric of Christianity: monotheism, and the worship of Jesus Christ as divine. Neither of these factors is specifically connected with Greek philosophy or thought; both arise directly from the earliest Christian tradition. Indeed, as will, it is hoped, be shown in this book, it was only by overcoming some tendencies in Greek philosophy which offered too easy an answer to the problem that a solution was reached. Greek philosophy and religion could readily accept a monotheism which included an hierarchically graded God and could easily accord a qualified divinity to the Son. Neither was in the end accepted by the Church. But it would of course be absurd to deny that discussion and dispute between 318 and 381 were conducted largely in terms of Greek philosophy. The reason for this was, paradoxically, because the dispute was about the interpretation of the Bible. The theologians of the Christian church were slowly driven to a realization that the deepest questions which face Christianity cannot be answered in purely biblical language, because the questions are about the meaning of biblical language itself. In the course of this search the church was impelled reluctantly to form dogma. It was the first great and authentic example of the development of doctrine. For theologians who are to-day interested in the subject of the development of doctrine, the study of the period from 318 to 381 should present an ideal case-history. This is another reason why the period is of permanent interest and importance" (pp. xx-xxi). For an excellent refutation of the thesis that Greek philosophy formed Christian doctrine, see Paul L. Gavrilyuk, *The Suffering of the Impassible God: The Dialectics of Patristic Thought* (Oxford: Oxford University Press, 2004), 21-46. Also see K. Scott Oliphint, *Reasons for Faith: Philosophy in the Service of Theology* (Phillipsburg, NJ: P&R Publishing, 2006).

person with an actualized theological ontology. Hodge sees this departure from the creed's *content* as a departure from Scripture. For Hodge to reject the creeds is to reject Scripture.

What was speculation for Hodge with regard to Christology? Before Hodge answers that he first states what is *not* christological speculation. It is the simple gospel taught in the New Testament "that the eternal Son of God became man by taking to Himself a true body and a reasonable soul, and so was and continues to be, God and man, in two entire distinct natures, and one person forever." Hodge clearly states, "Whatever is beyond this, is mere speculation. Not content with admitting the *fact* that two natures are united in the one person of Christ, the Lutheran theologians *insist on explaining that fact*." Hodge is writing this in the context of critiquing Lutheran Christology. According to him, the Lutherans were not content to just state the *fact* that two *distinct* natures are in one person. Hodge admits there is an unexplainable mystery here, but he sees the desire to "explain the inscrutable" as what is motivating the Lutherans to explain the problem of how one person can have two *distinct* natures. He laments that the Lutherans do this and asks, "Why then can they not receive the fact that two natures are united in Christ without philosophizing about it?" [173] In philosophizing about the bodily presence of Christ in the Lord's Supper, which was a distinctive Lutheran view, the Lutherans had an abstract view of the communication of properties from the divine to the human.[174] Hodge saw their view of bodily presence in communion as controlling their exegesis of

---

[173] Hodge, *Systematic Theology*, 2:413-14 (emphasis mine).
[174] For a full explanation of the *communicatio idiomatum* in Lutheran and Reformed theology, see Muller, *Dictionary of Latin and Greek Theological Terms*, 72-74.

Scripture.[175] The transfer of attributes from the divine to the human nature was a philosophical move and not based on sound exegetical principles of Scripture.

How does Hodge's critique of Lutheranism help us in evaluating McCormack's Christology? First, it helps us to see that any transfer of attributes from divine to human or vice versa is against Chalcedon. Second, there is a similarity between Lutheran Christology/modern Christology and McCormack's. There is a strong rational strain in McCormack that wants to make a positive contribution to the problem of God's immutability in relation to the incarnation. These three things are interrelated for McCormack: (1) theological ontology, (2) divine immutability, (3) incarnation (Christology). They are related for Hodge as well but with different theological presuppositions. We will now see how philosophical moves (also called theological by McCormack) work out a solution to the problem of immutability and how that contrasts with Hodge.

Theological Ontology Presupposed and Divine Immutability

As we have compared and contrasted Hodge with McCormack, theological ontology and divine immutability have been mentioned. We will explore their relationship in the context of Christology and see the contrast of a theology based on philosophical speculation (McCormack) vs. biblical authority (Hodge). [176] Though McCormack professes to not be speculative, it is our contention that his Christology is speculative.

---

[175] Hodge, *Systematic Theology*, 2:414.
[176] Ibid., 2:453.

Does Hodge's view of God's nature entail an essential change in God at the time of incarnation, and does Hodge's view of God's being entail a static, cold God who cannot relate to us? Hodge would confess with WSC 4 that "God is a Spirit, infinite, eternal, and unchangeable, in his being, wisdom, power, holiness, justice, goodness, and truth." God's being for Hodge is independent (*a se*) and complete in himself. Hodge would bring substance into this discussion as well, which he does when commenting on God's spirituality. He stresses that words must be interpreted in the historical context in which they are used and lists nuances for the word spirit (רוח and πνευμα) meaning "air," "breath," or "any invisible power; then the human soul." Hodge next does a type of *via eminentiae* (way of eminence) [177] which, for him, is subordinated to Scripture, but is rejected by McCormack. McCormack describes this method as learning who God is by looking first at things in the created order and then postulating of God things of a higher order. [178] We would agree with McCormack if this is done autonomously by humans, but done in subordination to the Bible it is a proper use of reason (thinking God's thoughts after him). Hodge explains his method this way: "In saying, therefore, that God is a Spirit, our Lord authorizes us to believe that whatever is essential to the idea of a spirit, as learned from our own consciousness, is to be referred to God as determining his nature." From what is "learned from our own consciousness" Hodge states that "the soul is a substance." Again, *substance* is a fundamental concept for Hodge as he explains:

---

[177] For an explanation of via eminentiae see Muller, *Dictionary of Latin and Greek Theological Terms*, 326.

[178] McCormack, "Actuality of God," 211-12.

> Substance is that which has an objective existence, and has permanence and power. Even Kant says:…where operation, and consequently activity and power are, there is substance. This is not only the common conviction of men, but it is admitted by the vast majority of philosophers. As before remarked, that there should be action without something acting, is as unthinkable as that there should be motion without something moving.[179]

Substance for Hodge does not denote something that is lifeless, cold, static, or unrelational. That God is a spirit means he is "a person—a self-conscious, intelligent, voluntary agent."[180] For him, God's substance (being) is eternal, independent, uncreated, infinite, complete, self-contained, and unchanging.[181] God is *"perpetually active,"* and the activity of God comes from his being (substance).[182] God's infinitude, immensity, eternality and immutability are interconnected.[183] He is convinced Scripture teaches there are no limits or "increases or decreases" on God's being, plan, or purpose and where we cannot reconcile difficulties (as philosophy has attempted) we submit to God's word:

> To give up the living, personal God of the Bible and of the heart, is an awful sacrifice to *specious logical consistency.* We believe what we cannot understand. We believe what the Bible teaches as facts; that God always is, was, and ever will be, immutably the same…but nevertheless that He is *not a stagnant* ocean, but ever living, ever thinking, ever acting, and ever suiting his action to the exigencies of his creatures, and to the accomplishment of his infinitely wise designs. Whether we can harmonize these facts

---

[179] Hodge, *Systematic Theology*, 1:377.
[180] Ibid., 1:379.
[181] Ibid., 1:392. See also WSC 4 and WCF 2:1.
[182] Ibid., 391 (emphasis mine).
[183] Ibid., 390.

or not, is a matter of minor importance. We are constantly called upon to believe that things are, *without being able to tell how they are*, or even how they can be.[184]

Hodge takes up the claim of theologians, guided by philosophy, that immutability means God is "immobile." While humans, thinking autonomously, have unbiblical assumptions and "arbitrary definitions" which make immutability and mobility "not compatible," Hodge goes to the Bible for his answer to the supposed impossibility. Since the Bible teaches both truths, that God is unchanging and yet acts, we know it is true and compatible.[185] Hodge appeals to Scripture, instead of speculative philosophy, which teaches that God alone is independent, necessary, self-complete, and subordinate to nothing outside himself. Hodge's epistemology is revelational and is inextricably tied to his metaphysics of God's immutable being.[186] He warns,

> We must abide by the teachings of Scripture, and refuse to subordinate their authority and the intuitive convictions of our moral and religious nature to the *arbitrary definitions* of any philosophical system. The Bible everywhere teaches that God is an absolute Being, in the sense of being self-existent, necessary, independent, immutable, eternal, and without limitation or necessary relation to anything out of Himself.[187]

McCormack claims that the Chalcedonian fathers' teaching of an eternal Son who took on flesh in time

---

[184] Hodge, *Systematic Theology*, 1:389-90 (emphasis mine).

[185] Ibid., 1:391-92.

[186] Cornelius Van Til saw inconsistencies between Hodge's theology and his epistemology; see Van Til, *An Introduction to Systematic Theology*, ch. 4.

[187] Hodge, *Systematic Theology*, 1:392.

involves a violation of divine immutability as described by Hodge above. In other words, a Metaphysical Subject, who is complete in himself, cannot take on contingent properties into his person without undergoing an essential change, according to McCormack. McCormack states that the "unseen guest" at the council of Chalcedon was *divine immutability.* He proposes a different "understanding" to divine immutability that is modern in its philosophical commitments and yet does not violate the "values" of Chalcedon.[188] McCormack believes this concern to answer the problem of immutability has been the "red thread" running throughout Barth's writings. [189] Would Hodge consider McCormack's understanding of immutability to be arbitrary, as he did in critiquing the philosophical theology of his day? Yes, and also *nonsensical* because of its rejection of substance.

Clarifications

With this discussion of immutability we have some matters to clarify. First, what is the different understanding of divine immutability that McCormack proposes? The difference is in how God's eternal essence is perceived. For McCormack, the essence of God is an Act, and specifically it is God's act where in Jesus Christ he decides eternally to be God *for us.* It is an act of "self-determination" according to McCormack, where God decides the being he will have for all eternity. In this scheme, God's very being is the act

---

[188] See McCormack, "The Ontological Presuppositions of Barth's Doctrine of the Atonement," 356-57. For an explanation of how Barth is modern in his philosophical commitments and still orthodox in his doctrine, see McCormack, *Orthodox and Modern*, 10-17.

[189] See McCormack, "The Being of Holy Scripture Is in Becoming," 74.

of incarnation—Jesus Christ. So, God's being has not undergone change because God has eternally decided to be Jesus Christ and continues to decide this (it is eternal). It is impossible for God not to decide this. In this line of thinking, God's being is eternally the God-human with human attributes of humility and obedience but also majestic.[190] This is the new understanding of immutability according to McCormack. It is a rejection of the *Logos asarkos* (without flesh) from all eternity who becomes *Logos ensarkos* (enfleshed) in time.

A second matter to clarify with this new definition of immutability is McCormack's unbiblical view of God's being. Hodge would call it pantheistic, meaning God and man are in essence the same. Hodge described the modern Christology of his day as confusing because it involved a mixture of pantheistic teaching with theistic teaching.[191] For McCormack "act" logically precedes God's being, but for Hodge, God's being is prior to "act." God's being for Hodge is *complete and self-sufficient* prior to any act, but for McCormack God's being is *not* complete and self-sufficient. For Hodge the modern McCormack proposal is contrary to the *facts* of Scripture which teaches that God's being is unchanging. Hodge would consider it arbitrary because it is changing terms to satisfy a rationalism that wants to solve

---

[190] See Bruce L. McCormack, "Divine Impassiblity or Simply Divine Constancy? Implications of Karl Barth's Later Christology for Debates over Impassiblilty," in *Divine Impassiblity and the Mystery of Human Suffering*, ed. James F. Keating and Thomas Joseph White, O.P. (Grand Rapids: William B. Eerdmans Publishing, 2009), 170-71.

[191] Concerning the mixing of philosophy with theology which brings confusion, Hodge says, "In the modern systems, however, there is such a blending of pantheistic principles with theistic doctrines, that the two cannot be kept entirely separate." See Hodge, *Systematic Theology*, 2:429.

the mystery of how one person (the eternal Son) can have two complete natures and still be one person.[192]

Every challenge McCormack brings against the biblical view of God being independent and complete in himself, before he decides to create or redeem, is based on modern philosophical presuppositions. These presuppositions assert that an eternally unchanging God cannot come to redeem his fallen creation by taking on created properties (human nature) without undergoing an essential change. McCormack would charge Hodge with a hopeless "vascillation between Apollinarianism and Nestorianism" because of his view of divine immutability and the incarnation of the eternal Son with a human nature.[193] With McCormack's philosophical commitments, the incarnation of the eternal Son, who is *a se,* is an impossibility. Hodge's response would be that God's word is never subordinate to human logic.[194] The problem with an unbiblical metaphysic (McCormack's), which views God's being as divine/human from all eternity, is a failure to submit one's presuppositions to what the Bible plainly teaches about God's being and the incarnation occurring in time and *not* from eternity.[195]

CONCLUSION

As we have seen, the Chalcedonian Christology of Hodge is deeply rooted in scriptural exegesis. Hodge took an anthropological analogy and used it as a faithful illustration of Christ's one person in two true natures (divine and human). His presuppositions were a commitment to God's

---

[192] Ibid., 2:398.
[193] McCormack, "The Ontological Presuppositions of Barth's Doctrine of the Atonement," 357.
[194] Hodge, *Systematic Theology*, 1:392.
[195] Ibid., 2:427.

inerrant word and God's being as absolutely complete and unchanging in himself. He held the creed of Chalcedon to be what the Bible clearly teaches about Christ's one person in two distinct natures. Furthermore, he saw *substance* as an important concept to use in explaining the distinctness of the divine and human natures. McCormack on the other hand has jettisoned this Chalcedonian tradition for a modern option which is seen by him as viable because philosophical commitments change with each age. [196] McCormack believes the concepts of terms such as *person* and *nature* can be fundamentally changed to be in agreement with modern philosophical commitments and still be true to the "values" of Chalcedon. This is putting Scripture in subordination to philosophy. The most devastating result of this move is the loss of a God who is *a se* (independent), complete in himself, and unchanging. The Reformed tradition, as represented by Hodge, gives a biblical way of maintaining the distinction of Christ's natures in one person while not sacrificing God's aseity and immutability. Hodge champions a robust Chalcedonian Christology which is founded on Scripture and not speculation. To replace Scripture with philosophy is to end up in uncertainty. Hodge reminds and warns the church with these words:

> As Christian theology is simply the exhibition and illustration of the facts and truths of the Bible in their

---

[196] McCormack's conviction concerning philosophy's role in theology and epistemology is "that all human thinking is conditioned by historical (and cultural) location—that was most basic to the emergence of what we tend to think of as 'modern' theology." The philosophies that McCormack believes shaped Barth were those of Kant, Herder, Hamann, and Hegel. See McCormack, *Orthodox and Modern*, 9-18. For a fuller treatment of Barth's historical, theological, and philosophical context, see Bruce L. McCormack, *Karl Barth's Critically Realistic Dialectical Theology: Its Genesis and Development, 1909-1936* (Oxford: Oxford University Press, 2004).

due relations and proportions, it has nothing to do with these speculations [Schleiermacher and modern Christology]….It avowedly gives up Christianity as a doctrine to save it as a life. It is founded on "speculation" and not upon authority, whether of the Scriptures or of the Church. It affords therefore no other and no firmer foundation for our faith and hope, than any other philosophical system; and that, as all history proves, is a *foundation of quick-sand*, shifting and sinking from month to month and even from day to day.[197]

Having looked at Hodge's Christology in contrast with that of McCormack, we will now look at the Chalcedonian Christology of Herman Bavinck (1854-1921) to glean his insights on articulating Chalcedonian Christology in a modern context.

---

[197] Hodge, *Systematic Theology*, 2:453 (emphasis mine).

CHAPTER 4

THE CHRISTOLOGY OF HERMAN BAVINCK: OLD AMSTERDAM SPEAKS

In the previous chapter we compared Hodge's Christology to McCormack's Barthian Christology and highlighted their similarities and differences. In this chapter we will compare and contrast McCormack's Christology with the Christology of a professor from old Amsterdam, Herman Bavinck (1854-1921). [198] Bavinck lived during the resurgence of Calvinism (Neo-Calvinism) in the Netherlands during the nineteenth century, and was one of its strongest proponents. His Christology is representative of the Reformed tradition (as was Hodge's), and this comparison with McCormack's Christology will underscore what is distinctive about a Reformed/Chalcedonian Christology. [199] While Hodge clearly defined Chalcedonian Christology and provided helpful contrasts, Bavinck's contribution will be unique in some areas and will strengthen Chalcedonian

---

[198] For biographical information on Herman Bavinck, see Ron Gleason, *Herman Bavinck: Pastor, Churchman, Statesman, and Theologian* (Phillipsburg, NJ: P&R Publishing, 2010).

[199] The terms Chalcedonian, Reformed, and orthodox are used interchangeably in this thesis.

Christology against the challenges McCormack's proposal brings.

Bavinck will be compared and contrasted with McCormack's Barthian Christology in these four areas: (1) the ground of Christ's deity (theological ontology), (2) one person Christology, (3) two natures in Christ, and (4) divine immutability. Within these four areas McCormack's concerns and criticisms will be examined with a Reformed reply by Bavinck. As we have seen, the "form" of the "two natures" Christology of McCormack is different from the Reformed/Chalcedonian Christology of Charles Hodge.[200] Our overarching question is the following: Is the form of the two natures Christology of Bruce McCormack Chalcedonian?

So, in addition to the four areas listed above, we will also look at two concerns McCormack raises about Chalcedonian Christology. The first is the communication of operations (*communicatio operationum*) which refers to the one person of Christ *acting* from two natures as is proper to each nature.[201] McCormack does not see how a Reformed Christology can rightly hold to one person in the way it assigns certain activities or experiences (such as hunger, sleep, fear, death) to the human nature, and other experiences and activities to the divine nature (creation,

---

[200] McCormack admits that his proposal of "two natures" Christology is in a different "form" than the Chalcedonian fathers; see Bruce L. McCormack, "Karl Barth's Christology as a Resource for a Reformed Version of Kenoticism," *International Journal of Systematic Theology* 8, no. 3 (July 2006): 251.

[201] Muller, *Dictionary of Latin and Greek Theological Terms*, 74-75. The *communicatio operationum* is also *communicatio apotelesmatum* ("the communication of mediatorial operations in and for the sake of the work of salvation"). Muller states that the communication of operations is a Reformed idea and that it "indicate[s] the common work of the two natures of Christ, each doing what is proper to it according to its own attributes" (ibid.).

providence, forgiveness). He sees this scheme as hopelessly vacillating between Apollinarianism and Nestorianism.[202] For McCormack, Chalcedonian Christology violates the unity of the person because it abstracts the human nature from the Logos (with a nature). This scheme makes subjects of both natures. According to McCormack, the human nature really does not belong to the Logos under this orthodox explanation.[203]

McCormack's second challenge to (or concern with) Chalcedonian Christology is the question of what is "controlling" its view of immutability. McCormack says it is "substantialist" thinking which posits a *Logos asarkos* (without flesh). His proposal is to abandon the *Logos asarkos* and to historicize the one person and identify it as the God-human.[204] We have already touched upon these subjects in the last chapter, but in this one we will use the Reformed Christology of Bavinck to answer McCormack's challenges.

THE GROUND OF CHRIST'S DEITY— THEOLOGICAL ONTOLOGY PRESUPPOSED

A unique point that Bavinck makes regarding Christology needs to be highlighted to frame our discussion from this point onward. He emphasizes that Christology is "not the starting point" in systematic theology but it is "central" to the task of systematics. All other doctrines either move toward it (by way of preparation) or flow from it (by way of implication). For Bavinck, Christology is "the heart of

---

[202] McCormack, "Ontological Presuppositions," 357.
[203] Ibid.
[204] Ibid., 357-58.

dogmatics."[205] From that initial statement, he lays out what are the three presuppositions for the incarnation of the eternal Son: (1) the ontological Trinity, (2) "creation," and (3) "the history of revelation." [206] Unbiblical views of "theology proper" such as Deism, Pantheism, Socianism, etc., either do not allow for the incarnation or consider it "absurd." The incarnation is only possible with the ontological Trinity: "Only the theistic trinitarian confession of God's characteristic essence opens the *possibility* for the fact of the incarnation. For here God remains who he is and can yet communicate himself to others."[207] Bavinck's ordering of these three presuppositions is logical, because before creation all that existed was the triune God—Father, Son, and Holy Spirit.

God's triune essence is *not becoming* but is "absolute" and "personal" being. [208] "Absolute" is not taken in the philosophical sense of "without limits" but in a biblical sense meaning "that which is not dependent on anything else."[209] That God is "personal" means he is relational in himself among the three persons (*ad intra*) and also with his creation (*ad extra*). Bavinck does not have a philosophical dualism that maintains a metaphysical barrier between God and his creation that cannot be crossed. The personal, absolute, triune God, who alone is necessary, is able to relate to his creation, and he does so by way of the covenant of redemption among the divine persons (*pactum*

---

[205] Herman Bavinck, *Reformed Dogmatics*, vol. 3, *Sin and Salvation in Christ*, ed. John Bolt, trans. John Vriend (Grand Rapids: Baker Academic, 2006), 274.

[206] Ibid., 3:274-82.

[207] Ibid., 3:274-75 (emphasis mine).

[208] Herman Bavinck, *Reformed Dogmatics*, vol. 2, *God and Creation*, ed. John Bolt, trans. John Vriend (Grand Rapids: Baker Academic, 2004), 34, 47, 49.

[209] Ibid., 2:123, 49. Bavinck is quoting J. Alsted (p. 123).

salutus). The second person of the ontological Trinity is the mediator and surety of the covenant from eternity, and is so because of God's one decree.[210] It is crucial to Bavinck's theology that the incarnation is not accidental to God's one eternal plan. This would violate God's sovereignty and immutability.[211]

Since God's being is absolute, creation and the incarnation are not necessary. There is no ontological reason for these two events.[212] God in himself (*in se*) is complete and satisfied. "God is independent, all sufficient in himself, and the only source of all existence and life."[213] All of God's activities outside himself (*ad extra*) are based on his free will.[214] In contrast to Bavinck, McCormack believes God's being is *not* complete before his decision to redeem. He sees the one event of redemption as constitutive of God's being. As we saw earlier, election is the *basis* for God's being. For McCormack, Jesus Christ is both the subject and object of election, and God's being is constituted by this one covenantal event *for us*.[215] McCormack has a different methodology and a different theological ontology. His method is to *start* with Jesus Christ which is the foundation for God's being in eternity.[216] Bavinck, by contrast, starts with the ontological

---

[210] Ibid., 3:275-77.

[211] Ibid., 3:278-79.

[212] Ibid.

[213] Ibid., 2:148.

[214] For an explanation of God's necessary and free will, see ibid., 2:229-35.

[215] McCormack, "Actuality of God," 213-19. Also see McCormack, *Orthodox and Modern*, 190.

[216] McCormack in following Barth is involved in a "Christomonism" which starts and builds their entire theological structure on Jesus Christ. For an explanation of Christomonism, see Van Til, *An Introduction to Systematic Theology*, 16n5. Van Til prefers saying "God-

Trinity which is itself complete and the foundation for the economic Trinity in time. The entire Trinity is involved in all works toward creation (*ad extra*). Bavinck uniquely sees the incarnation, creation, revelation, and the outpouring of the Spirit as reflecting in time the internal incommunicable relations of the ontological Trinity from eternity. [217] He helpfully explains how the eternal relations of the persons are foundational and "mirrored" in time:

> But this "being sent" in time is a reflection of the immanent relations of the three persons in the divine being and is grounded in generation and spiration. The incarnation of the Word has its eternal archetype in the generation of the Son, and the outpouring of the Holy Spirit is a weak analogy of the procession from the Father and the Son.[218]

The ground for the deity of Jesus Christ, according to Bavinck, is that he *is* the eternal Son of God, meaning that he is unique and that he shares in the one divine essence of the Trinity. This unique Son, the second person of the Trinity, has existed from all eternity and is coequal with the Father and the Spirit in essence. While the modern Christology of Bavinck's day was abandoning a metaphysical Son, Bavinck, because of his scriptural/confessional moorings, was not convinced of this modern move. As Bavinck looks at the Scriptures he sees that the term "Son of God" has a unique meaning when referring to Jesus Christ:

> But Jesus invests it ["Son of God"] with another and deeper meaning. He is the Son of God not because

---

centered" instead of "Christ-centered" in describing systematic theology.
[217] Bavinck, *Reformed Dogmatics*, 2:318.
[218] Ibid., 2:320.

he is Messiah and king, but he is king because he is the Messiah, because he is the Son of the Father. God is his father (Luke 2:49); he is the only Son, whom the Father loved and whom he sent as his last emissary (Mark 12:6)....He already existed before his incarnation (John 1:1; 17:5; 1 Cor. 10:4, 9; Heb. 11:26) and was then "in the form of God" (Phil. 2:6)...the Son of God in an utterly unique sense (John 1:14; 5:18; Rom. 8:3, 32; Gal. 4:4) and himself God (John 1:1; 20:28; Rom. 9:5; 1 Thess. 1:1; Titus 2:13; Heb. 1:8-9 [1 John 5:20], 2 Pet. 1:1).[219]

The modern Christology of Bavinck's time would call Jesus God by way of a title, "status," or "rank" but *not* in his being.[220] For Bavinck, Jesus is God in his being, and this being is equally shared by each person of the ontological Trinity. The term "Son of God" clearly means "in a metaphysical sense: by nature and from eternity."[221] While the Son is equal to the Father in essence, he is distinguished from the Father in "his position and office." In his state of humiliation it is proper to say of the Son that "he is presently less than the Father."[222] Bavinck distinguishes the divine "persons" in the Trinity from the divine "being" (essence), and stresses that it is the eternal Son who took on flesh and *not* the divine essence of the Trinity. This detail of differentiation in the Godhead is critical for there to be reconciliation between God and man, as Bavinck states: "In a word, the Trinity makes possible the existence of a mediator who himself participates both in the divine and human nature and thus unites God and humans...[and] it is also important, therefore, to maintain that not the divine

---

[219] Ibid., 3:252-53.
[220] Ibid., 3:264-65.
[221] Ibid., 2:275.
[222] Ibid., 2:276.

nature as such but specifically the person of the Son became a human."[223]

ONE PERSON CHRISTOLOGY

As we have seen for Bavinck, Jesus Christ preexisted from all eternity and is consubstantial with the Father and the Spirit. Bavinck believes the Son is distinguished from the Father by an eternal begetting and that the incarnation is possible because of these presuppositions.[224] We are now considering the identity of the one person. For Bavinck, the identity of the one person who took on human nature is a divine person.[225] While the Reformed doctrine has been charged with Nestorianism, it has "avoided" this error by stressing the incarnation of the divine *person* and *not* the divine nature (being).[226] This was done to make it clear that there was no mixture of the two natures.[227] The whole Trinity was involved in the decision of incarnation as well as that of salvation (*pactum salutis*). So the subject of election for Bavinck was not the Son alone but the Trinity. In that pact (the covenant of redemption), the Son agreed to take on human flesh and be the mediator of a chosen people. All this happened in eternity past before creation. Bavinck distinguishes "origin" from goal or "end" with respect to the incarnation in the Trinity.

> Yet though subjectively and as it pertains to its end, the incarnation is peculiar to the Son, still with respect to its origin, beginning, and effectiveness, *it is the work of the whole Trinity*....The entire work of re-

---

[223] Ibid., 3:275.
[224] Ibid., 3:304.
[225] Ibid., 3:275, 307.
[226] Ibid., 3:259.
[227] Ibid.

creation is not just a decree of God; it is rooted in the free and conscious consultation of the three persons. It is a personal, not a natural, work. In the Son, the Father is from all eternity the Father of his children; the Son is eternally their guarantor and mediator; the Holy Spirit is eternally their Comforter. Not just after the fall, not even first at the creation, but in eternity the foundations of the covenant of grace were laid. And the incarnation is not an incidental decree that emerged later: it was decided and determined from eternity. There was no time when the Son did not exist; there was also no time when the Son did not know he would assume and when he was not prepared to assume the human nature from the fallen race of Adam. The incarnation was prepared from eternity; it does not rest in the essence of God but in the person. It is not a necessity as in pantheism, but neither is it arbitrary or accidental as in Pelagianism.[228]

As we saw earlier, McCormack levels this charge of Nestorianism against Chalcedonian/Reformed Christology.[229] Bavinck gives an answer based on careful attention to the details of Scripture: "Every moment in Scripture, divine as well as human predicates are attributed to the same personal subject: divine and human existence, omnipresence and [geographical] limitation, eternity and time, creative omnipotence and creaturely weakness. What else is this but the church's doctrine of the two natures united in one person?"[230] So, it is the one person of Christ who exhibits qualities that reflect both natures. Scriptural examples are "even though walking about on earth, he still continues to be 'in the bosom of the Father' (John 1:18),

---

[228] Ibid., 3:276-77 (emphasis mine).
[229] McCormack, "Actuality of God," 220, 222.
[230] Bavinck, *Reformed Dogmatics*, 3:298-99.

'the one who is in heaven' (John 3:13)."[231] The Reformed doctrine emphasizes one person acting from two distinct natures which retain their peculiar properties. What Reformed theologians have relied upon when accused of Nestorianism is an axiom based on a strict Creator/creature distinction. Bavinck emphasizes how the Reformed used this axiom: "While rigorously maintaining the unity of the person, they applied the rule 'the finite is not capable of [containing] the infinite' also to the human nature of Christ and maintained this rule not only in the state of humiliation but even in that of Christ's exaltation."[232] The Reformed distinctive that it is the "person" who is incarnate and *not* the divine nature, is crucial to maintaining a proper unity of person and a distinction of natures: "it was the *person* of the Son who became flesh—not the *substance* [the underlying reality] but the *subsistence* [the particular being] of the Son assumed our nature. The unity of the two natures, despite the sharp distinction between them is unalterably anchored in the person."[233] Bavinck is guarding against the Lutheran tendency to abstract the divine nature from the person, and so he is stressing the "person," but it is never a person without a nature. That is an impossibility.

---

[231] Ibid., 3:298.

[232] Ibid., 3:258, 259.

[233] Ibid., 3:259. Bavinck explains why the Reformed placed such an emphasis on the person and not the nature assuming flesh. He further states, "As it does in the doctrine of the Trinity, of humanity in the image of God, and of the covenants, so here in the doctrine of Christ as well, the Reformed idea of *conscious personal life as the fullest and highest life* comes dramatically to the fore" (ibid.; emphasis mine).

COMMUNICATION OF OPERATIONS AND THE HYPOSTATIC UNION

By distinguishing the two natures and yet attributing all the works of Christ to the one person how can Bavinck avoid the charge of Nestorianism? [234] Specifically, how would Bavinck answer McCormack's evaluation "that the commitment to impassibility also had the unintended effect of driving even the most ardent defenders of a single-Subject Christology in the direction of Nestorianism....Where the sufferings of Jesus are assigned to the human nature alone, there the human nature is being treated as if it were a Subject in its own right—which has to render incoherent the commitment to a single-Subject Christology." [235] Using Bavinck's Christology, the reply would attribute Jesus' death to the one person with reference to his human nature, which alone is able to suffer and die. Bavinck also sees the one person of Christ in a "personal" union with the human nature as opposed to a moral union of persons. [236] Additionally, in singling out different events in Christ's life to one of his natures, the Creator/creature distinction is upheld, which is critical in Reformed theology.[237] God in his essence cannot die, but God the eternal Son who assumed our nature died with reference to that nature, which was united to the divine

---

[234] Ibid., 3:304-8.

[235] McCormack, "Actuality of God," 220.

[236] Bavinck, *Reformed Dogmatics*, 3:305. Bavinck says the union of the two natures is "personal," "substantial," and "natural." He further says, "In virtue of its wholly unique nature, this union can only be conceived as a union of the person of the Son with an *impersonal* human nature. For if the human nature in Christ had its own personal existence, no union other than a moral one would have been possible" (ibid.; emphasis mine).

[237] Ibid., 2:156.

person who is fully God. There is mystery here but not contradiction. Bavinck makes a helpful point, in the context of revelation, which applies to the incarnation, and answers the charge of incoherence and contradiction:

> Here, indeed, lies something of an antinomy. Rather, agnosticism, suffering from a confusion of concepts, sees here an irresolvable contradiction in what Christian theology regards as an adorable mystery. It is completely incomprehensible to us how God can reveal himself and to some extent make himself known in created beings: eternity in time, immensity in space, infinity in the finite, immutability in change, being in becoming, the all, as it were, in that which is nothing. This mystery cannot be comprehended; it can only be gratefully acknowledged. *But mystery and self-contradiction are not synonymous.*[238]

Bavinck is going as far as Scripture allows, but this will not satisfy the philosophical presuppositions of McCormack's Christology which rejects the *Logos asarkos*.

TWO NATURES IN CHRIST

We have seen that Bavinck assumes and affirms the full deity of Christ, meaning Christ has all the essential attributes of God. McCormack, on the other hand, rejects this identity of Christ's person. He has redefined the deity of Christ. This new definition is detected when McCormack questions how the orthodox can genuinely hold to Christ's full deity when they maintain a distinction between the two natures. He asks, "How coherent can one's affirmation of the deity of Jesus Christ be if his being as Mediator is only accidentally related to what he is as Logos in and for

---

[238] Ibid., 2:49 (emphasis mine).

himself? Is Jesus Christ 'fully God' or not?" [239] For McCormack, the Logos without flesh is not fully divine and this affirmation by the Reformed amounts to *mythology*. He dogmatically claims that "any talk of the eternal Son in abstraction from the humanity to be assumed is an exercise in mythologizing; there is no such eternal son—and there never was." [240] The difference between McCormack and Bavinck is "at the level of divine ontology." [241] McCormack's theological ontology rejects an absolute metaphysical subject, and Bavinck's theological ontology, based on Scripture, sees God's being as independent (*a se*) before the incarnation in time. Listen to what Bavinck says about the deity of Christ as it relates to the essence of God which is *a se* and personal:

> Furthermore, the Christian church, in calling Jesus "God," meant it to be a reference never to his office but always to his *characteristic essence*. When people begin to use the same word and the same name in a totally different sense, they deliberately sow misunderstanding and confusion and act unfairly toward the church. Further, if Christ is not God in any *essential sense*, then neither may be called "God" or venerated as God....To be one with God in a religious and ethical sense is something totally different from being one with God in a *metaphysical sense*.[242]

While Bavinck has a different manifestation of modern Christology in mind than McCormack's, in principle they are the same in that they both reject the *Logos asarkos*. The

---

[239] McCormack, *Orthodox and Modern*, 188.
[240] McCormack, "Actuality of God," 218-19.
[241] McCormack, *Orthodox and Modern*, 189.
[242] Bavinck, *Reformed Dogmatics*, 3:285.

stakes are high here, for if Christ is not God (essentially *a se*) then he cannot be worshipped or be our redeemer.

> It is also clear that the Christian religion, that is, the true fellowship between God and humans, can be maintained in no other way than by the confession of the deity of Christ. For if Christ is not truly God, he is only a human being. And however highly he may be placed, he can neither in his person nor in his work be the content and object of the Christian faith.[243]

Bavinck's Christology has upheld Jesus' full and complete deity, but what about a full and complete humanity? Bavinck sees the necessity of Christ being truly human or he could not be our redeemer.[244] To prove the importance of Christ having a real and complete human nature, Bavinck quotes twice from John of Damascus: "For the whole Christ assumed the whole me that he might grant salvation to the whole me, for what is unassumable is incurable."[245] Bavinck affirms that Christ was a real human in every sense, except for sin, and that "the denial of the true and complete human nature always results from a certain dualism."[246] If dualism were true, which it is not, there could be no "true communion between God and humanity, God and the world, creation and re-creation, nature and grace, the eternal and the temporal." [247] He makes a striking statement regarding the importance of Christ being truly human and not a generic, plural humanity. He writes this in opposition to a pantheistic

---

[243] Ibid., 3:284.
[244] Ibid., 3:295-98. Bavinck devotes a section to Christ's human nature titled "Christ's True Humanity."
[245] Ibid., 3:297.
[246] Ibid.
[247] Ibid.

conception of the incarnation which would see the incarnation as necessary:[248]

> If God cannot become man in one person, neither can he do so in all persons. Against this dualistic and atomistic viewpoint, Scripture posits the organic one. In the one, God comes to all, not in appearance but in reality. There is one mediator between God and human kind, Christ Jesus, himself human [1 Tim. 2:5]. *But for that very reason his true and complete humanity is as important as his deity.*[249]

It is critical that Christ's human nature have everything ours has, except sin: "Even [if] one essential constituent in the human nature of Christ is excluded from true union and communion with God, there is [then] an element in creation that remains dualistically alongside and opposed to God...for what is unassumable is incurable."[250] Because Bavinck grounds the incarnation in the Trinity, which is "exhaustively personal" and communicative, there is the possibility of the eternal Son taking on creative properties.[251] Only with the presupposition of the ontological Trinity can there be an incarnation and a real relationship with God. Also, Bavinck is not saying there is a parity between the divine and human natures. In line with

---

[248] Ibid., 3:277. Bavinck says, "The incarnation was prepared from eternity; it does not rest in the essence of God but in the person. It is not a necessity as in pantheism, but neither is it arbitrary or accidental as in Pelagianism" (ibid.).

[249] Ibid., 3:298 (emphasis mine). "Organic" is a "key term" in understanding Bavinck's theology according to Gleason. See Gleason, *Herman Bavinck*, 162n30.

[250] Bavinck, *Reformed Dogmatics*, 3:298.

[251] "Exhaustively personal" is a term used by Lane G. Tipton that I believe reflects Bavinck's view of the personal relations among the divine persons. See Lane G. Tipton, "The Triune Personal God: Trinitarian Theology in the Thought of Cornelius Van Til" (PhD diss., Westminster Theological Seminary, 2004), 141.

Chalcedon, he sees the divine as primary and the human as secondary. Lane Tipton, in accordance with Bavinck's thought, clarifies the relationship between the natures; he explains that "we must always maintain that the eternal person of the Son of God remains the primary theological category. *The divine and human in the God-man therefore are not equally ultimate, existing in some sort of parity with one another. The divine is primary; the human, while real, is subordinate.*"[252]

It is this very notion of divine primacy and human subordination that McCormack cannot abide. For him, if there is no parity of the two natures then the human is serving the divine and this indicates that the human nature is incomplete and not free. As he would express it, "the human nature is reduced to the status of a passive instrument in the hands of the Logos; it is the object upon which the Logos acts…[and] if the mind and will that are proper to Christ's human nature do not cooperate fully and freely in every work of the God-human, then Christ's humanity was not full and complete after all." [253] McCormack's solution is to have the God-man do his works "humanly" in "dependence" upon the Holy Spirit and not through the Logos exerting "influence" over the human nature. [254] There are some Reformed theologians who share McCormack's concern that divine primacy makes any talk about a real human activity by Christ's singular person incoherent.[255] Bavinck, on the other hand,

---

[252] Lane G. Tipton, "The Presence of Divine Persons: Extending the Incarnational Analogy to Impeccability and Inerrancy," *The Confessional Presbyterian* 6 (2010): 197 (italics in original).

[253] McCormack, "Ontological Presuppositions," 352-53.

[254] Ibid., 353.

[255] See Joel R. Beeke and Mark Jones, *A Puritan Theology: Doctrine for Life* (Grand Rapids: Reformation Heritage Books, 2012), 339, where Beeke and Jones share a similar concern when Christ's one person is identified as divine: "Thus, for Cyril, the Logos acts as the agent of all

in holding to a Creator/creature distinction, sees the divine as primary and the human as subordinate in Christ's person. He affirms asymmetry with the two natures because if they are symmetrical in status and relationship, then there is no proper metaphysical distinction between the triune God and his creation. Based on his presupposition of the ontological Trinity this is an impossibility. After he quotes from Aquinas (who clearly teaches that the divine person is greater than the human nature being added), he says Christ remains a divine person after the incarnation. Bavinck does not confess to Christ's person being complex:[256]

> Accordingly, the human nature in Christ is *not coordinated* with the Logos by a personality of its own but *subordinated* to the Logos. The two natures, indeed, are and remain "one thing and [then] another" (ἀλλο και ἀλλο), but *not* "one person and [then] another" (ἀλλος και ἀλλος). It is always the same person, the same subject, the same "I," who lives and thinks, speaks and acts through the divine and the human nature. The human nature is the tent in which the Son assumes residence; the garment that

---

that is done in the human nature, a position that raises a host of problems, including how the integrity of the human nature could be preserved. In other words, how can we speak of truly human experiences? Moreover, ascribing suffering to the Logos while affirming divine impassibility proves to be, at best, incoherent. Consequently, following Leo the Great (c. 391-461), Reformed theologians have used the idea of 'person' to refer to Christ in both His natures and not the Logos only (*simpliciter*). The incarnation resulted in a 'complex person,' one that reflects the two natures of the God-man, Jesus Christ."

[256] Some Reformed theologians, such as Louis Berkhof, William G. T. Shedd, Joel R. Beeke, and Mark Jones, confess that the person of Christ is "complex," meaning that with the incarnation the person is now the God-man. See Beeke and Jones, *A Puritan Theology*, 337-39; Louis Berkhof, *Systematic Theology* (1958; repr., Edinburgh: Banner of Truth Trust, 1998), 322; William G. T. Shedd, *Dogmatic Theology*, 3rd ed. (Phillipsburg, NJ: Presbyterian and Reformed, 2003), 615.

he himself prepared and put on; the form (μορφη) in which he has appeared to us; the instrument and organ that he has consecrated for himself and that, with divine wisdom, he employs for his office and work. "The human nature in Christ must be considered as though it were a kind of organ of the divine nature."[257]

Following Aquinas, Bavinck employs the word "organ" to refer to the human nature of Christ as well as "tent," "garment," "form," "instrument." In each of these analogies the divine person of Christ is working "through" a tool (human nature). For Bavinck, Christ is the creator and owner of the human nature; therefore, the human nature cannot be on a par with the divine nature. The human nature is a servant of the divine person of Christ, just as all of creation freely serves the Creator.[258] Bavinck sees no violation of the will of Christ's human nature when it acts in accordance with, and is in an inseparable union with, the one divine person (and nature). Bavinck asks with regard to the human nature serving the divine person (and nature):

> Then what objection would there be to the idea that in an even much greater measure—in an absolute sense—the human nature in Christ is the splendid, willing organ of his deity? How utterly the mystery of the union of the divine and human nature in Christ exceeds all our speaking and thinking of it. All comparison breaks down, for it is without equal.[259]

While we employ human analogies to explain the relations of the two natures to one another, we still have to end our theological investigation with mystery,

---

[257] Bavinck, *Reformed Dogmatics*, 3:307 (emphasis mine).
[258] Ibid., 3:307.
[259] Ibid., 3:307-8.

incomprehensibility, and worship of Christ, for this unique event of incarnation will never be repeated and is the mystery of godliness.[260]

THE IMMUTABILITY OF GOD

All these discussions above are related to God's immutability. As we saw in the previous chapters, McCormack has *redefined* what the immutability of God is in relation to the incarnation. McCormack believes Chalcedonian Christology is stuck in an "impossible" situation because, as he puts it, it is committed to a Greek substantialist metaphysic that identifies the one person who incarnates in time as the *Logos asarkos* (Word without flesh). Barth, according to McCormack, was concerned his entire career to preserve the godness of God with regard to the incarnation. Barth saw Chalcedon's insistence on the eternal Son (*Logos asarkos*) as being the one who takes on flesh into his person, as a violation of God's immutability as defined by the Chalcedonian fathers, and so, God's godness is sacrificed, according to McCormack.[261]

For Bavinck God's immutability is essential to his being God. "If God were not immutable, he would not be God."[262] It is in the doctrine of immutability where the Creator/creature distinction is clearly seen. The Creator is "being" and cannot change in his essence. "Absolute being is because it is. The idea of God itself implies immutability."[263] Conversely, the creature is characterized by "becoming" and does change. "Becoming is an attribute

---

[260] Ibid., 3:308.
[261] See McCormack, "Actuality of God," 222-23.
[262] Bavinck, *Reformed Dogmatics*, 2:154.
[263] Ibid., 2:158.

of creatures, a form of change in space and time."[264] God, who alone is *a se* (independent), is "being" and never "becoming." Bavinck explains, "The difference between the Creator and the creature hinges on the contrast between being and becoming. All that is creaturely is in process of becoming....We humans can rely on him; he does not change in his being, knowing, or willing."[265] So when the second Person of the Trinity, who has all the essential characteristics of God, takes on human flesh in time, does that constitute an essential change in God? No, Bavinck sees the change that happened with the Son assuming human flesh in time to be a *real* change with a creaturely addition (i.e. assumed human flesh) to the divine person, but *not* an essential change to God's being.[266] God's being alone is necessary and cannot suffer change in any way. The distinction of the Creator from the creature helps us to explain how a real change could occur (by way of addition) but not an essential change to Christ in the incarnation. There is mystery here with the uniqueness of the eternal Son taking on something creaturely that will now be with him throughout eternity, but no contradiction or mere "role play" has occurred.[267] If the incarnation made an essential

---

[264] Ibid.

[265] Ibid., 2:156.

[266] Ibid., 2:158. Bavinck says, "Those who predicate any change whatsoever of God, whether with respect to his essence, knowledge, or will, diminish all his attributes: independence, simplicity, eternity, omniscience, and omnipotence. This robs God of his divine nature, and religion of its firm foundation and assured comfort" (ibid.). Also see K. Scott Oliphint, *Reasons for Faith: Philosophy in the Service of Theology* (Phillipsburg, NJ: P&R Publishing, 2006), 191-255. Oliphint explains and uses "the Eimi/eikon metaphysical structure" to answer the hard questions related to God's immutability as he relates to his creation (249).

[267] See Oliphint, *Reasons for Faith*, 233-55. In the pages listed Oliphint shows how God relates to his creation without violating who he is

change to Christ, which it did not, then God has changed (in his nature), which is impossible for him to do. For Bavinck, who is solidly rooted in Scripture, the Creator/creature distinction has been established by the triune God and cannot be violated.

For McCormack, the identity of the Logos is connected with the immutability of God. We would agree but in a different way. McCormack's proposal is to identify the one person as the God-man. As we have seen, some Reformed theologians maintain that position (Berkhof and Shedd), but their view of Christ's person is substantially different from McCormack's, and for them it is *not* the basis for God's eternal being as it is for McCormack. One of the things McCormack is concerned with in this connection is applying the creedal boundaries of the two wills in Christ, which were affirmed at the sixth Ecumenical Council (A.D. 681). He quotes from the Council: "two natural volitions or wills in Him and two natural principles of action which undergo no division, no change, no partition, no confusion." McCormack sees the creed's meaning as self-evident and believes the "no confusion" and "no change" with regard to Christ's wills is not violated by many, but the

---

essentially. See especially pp. 245-47 on the incarnation. See also K. Scott Oliphint, *God With Us: Divine Condescension and the Attributes of God* (Wheaton, IL: Crossway, 2012), ch. 3. See McCormack, *Orthodox and Modern*, 188. McCormack characterizes the orthodox position of incarnation as "a role which he [the Logos] plays" (ibid.). Also see Bavinck, *Reformed Dogmatics*, 3:304-5. Though the incarnation is unique Bavinck explains, "yet it is intimately connected with everything that took place before, alongside and after itself." Bavinck is referring to the Trinity, "creation," "revelation," "inspiration," and now he adds "religion" which he defines as "communion with God" (3:304). Bavinck then shows the connection of God's covenant with the incarnation with Christ as our representative, the second Adam (3:305).

"no division" and "no partition" is often violated. He explains the violation this way:

> The tendency of the overwhelming majority of theologians from the ancient church right on through the Reformation was to parcel out the work of Christ to the "natures" in such a way that some actions were assigned to the divine nature and some to the human nature alone. Where this occurred, the "natures" were made "subjects" in their own right. The singularity of the subject of these natures was lost to view—and with that, the unity of the work.[268]

In response to McCormack, the creed is mirroring the Chalcedonian distinctions where the properties of each nature are preserved—*without confusion, change, separation, or division.* Louis Berkhof says the sixth Ecumenical Council of Constantinople taught "that the human will must always be conceived as subordinate to the divine...[and] the two [wills are] always acting in perfect harmony."[269] How this occurs the orthodox cannot explain. McCormack cites Calvin in *Institutes* 2.14.2 as an example of this parceling out the works of Christ to the different natures. He agrees with Calvin that humans suffer, but is silent when Calvin states that God does not suffer. It seems that McCormack cannot conceive of a divine person (with a nature and will) acting in accordance with the human nature he assumed in time. In commenting on Calvin, McCormack states, "But if this human nature is not a subject in its own right [as Calvin maintains], then how can we fail to assign such acts and experiences to the one subject in whom this nature is given its existence? The Logos clothed in his human nature is the subject who performs all aspects of the reconciling and

---

[268] McCormack, "Ontological Presuppositions," 354.
[269] Louis Berkhof, *The History of Christian Doctrines* (1939; repr., Edinburgh: Banner of Truth Trust, 2009), 110.

redemptive work; there is no other subject." [270] Bavinck would agree; the Logos is the one subject who acts in accordance with both natures in one common work. "Scripture ascribes all kinds of and very different predicates to Christ but always to one and the same subject, the one undivided 'I' who dwells in him and speaks out of him."[271] Bavinck in stressing the one person acting out of both natures appeals to John 1:14 and stresses that the Word "became flesh" as opposed to the Word "indwelling" a human body. Another point he makes is based on the axiom, "a person is what he or she has become." While many qualities may describe what a person becomes, "another person" is never one of those qualities.[272] In sum, Bavinck and Calvin properly distinguish the natures *without separating* (abstracting) them from the one person, but it is at this point that McCormack's presuppositions, which mix the divine and the human and reject the eternal Son (*Logos asarkos*), will not allow him to do the same. But, what does this discussion have to do with immutability?

McCormack believes divine immutability along with divine impassibility is motivating theologians, like Calvin, to parcel out the activities of the two natures as just described. A charge of violating immutability is advanced on both sides. Bavinck viewed any mixing of the two natures of Christ (as McCormack has done) as a violation of divine immutability. He says, "The Monophysite and kenotic doctrine is at odds with the immutability of God, with all the attributes and the essence of God, and similarly with the nature of the creature, of the finite being."[273]

---

[270] McCormack, "Ontological Presuppositions," 354n11.
[271] Bavinck, *Reformed Dogmatics*, 3:302.
[272] Ibid.
[273] Ibid., 3:303.

CONCLUSION

We want to end where we started, with the ontological Trinity. McCormack claims that the orthodox assume a "substantialist" way of thinking with regard to God's being in relationship to immutability. Following Bavinck, Reformed Christology does presuppose the personal, absolute, self-complete ontological Trinity. Bavinck would reject the static Parmenidean notion of substance because it is based on man's autonomous reason and not Scripture.

In this discussion on Chalcedonian Christology, Bavinck has given us a unique contribution. It is seen in his emphasis on the presupposition of the ontological Trinity for the incarnation, and for grounding not only the incarnation, but also creation and revelation. Bavinck has highlighted the Reformed distinctive and contribution necessary to develop a robust Chalcedonian Christology, which is *God's absolute personal consciousness*.[274] This Reformed distinctive will be used in our critique of McCormack's form of two natures Christology. Next in this critique, we will use the resources of Cornelius Van Til, who constructed and advanced his theology on the foundations of Old Amsterdam and Old Princeton.

---

[274] See ibid., 3:259. Bavinck states, "As it does in the doctrine of the Trinity, of humanity in the image of God, and of the covenants, so here in the doctrine of Christ as well, the Reformed idea of *conscious personal life* as the fullest and highest life comes dramatically to the fore" (emphasis mine).

CHAPTER 5

CORNELIUS VAN TIL'S CRITIQUE

Having just compared and contrasted Bavinck's Christology with McCormack's Christology we will continue using Bavinck's insights in conjunction with another Dutchman, Cornelius Van Til (1895-1987). It is fitting that we do so, because Van Til's constructive context for doing theology included Bavinck's Reformed theology. This thesis is an examination of the Barthian Christology of Bruce McCormack, who has unashamedly used Barth as a resource in his constructive theology. We will now critique his form of two natures Christology using the insights of these Dutchmen to underscore what is Reformed Christology. But, why Van Til? First, Van Til is Reformed in his theology and was mentored by professors from both old Princeton and old Amsterdam. [275] Second, Van Til's

---

[275] For a helpful biography in understanding Van Til, see John R. Muether, *Cornelius Van Til: Reformed Apologist and Churchman* (Phillipsburg, NJ: Presbyterian and Reformed, 2008). For an understanding of his theology, see John M. Frame, *Cornelius Van Til: An Analysis of His Thought* (Phillipsburg, NJ: Presbyterian and Reformed, 1995). For a first-hand reading of Van Til's theology, see Cornelius Van Til, *An Introduction to Systematic Theology: Prolegomena and the Doctrines of Revelation, Scripture, and God,* ed. William Edgar (Phillipsburg, NJ: Presbyterian and Reformed, 2007). For his theology

entire academic career was spent reading and critiquing Barth.[276] Third and last, Van Til's interpretation of Barth is close to McCormack's. In fact, I believe Van Til's take on Barth is validated by McCormack, especially to the degree each sees actualism (historicism) and redemption as architectonic to his theological system.[277] The critique that follows will be in two categories: (1) theological ontology presupposed, and (2) two natures Christology.

THEOLOGICAL ONTOLOGY PRESUPPOSED

While McCormack and Van Til have differences over interpreting Barth, there are two major areas of agreement.[278] The first is in the area of epistemology where

---

and apologetic method, see Cornelius Van Til, *Christian Apologetics*, ed. William Edgar, 2nd ed. (Phillipsburg, NJ: Presbyterian and Reformed, 2003); Cornelius Van Til, *The Defense of the Faith*, ed. K. Scott Oliphint, 4th ed. (Phillipsburg, NJ: Presbyterian and Reformed, 2008).

[276] For Van Til's two major works on Barth, see Cornelius Van Til, *Christianity and Barthianism* (Phillipsburg, NJ: Presbyterian and Reformed, 1962); Cornelius Van Til, *The New Modernism: An Appraisal of the Theology of Barth and Brunner*, 2nd ed. (Philadelphia: Presbyterian and Reformed, 1947).

[277] See McCormack, *Orthodox and Modern*, 202.

[278] McCormack has written a critique of Van Til's critique of Barth. See Bruce L. McCormack, "Afterword: Reflections on Van Til's Critique of Barth," in *Karl Barth and American Evangelism*, ed. Bruce L. McCormack and Clifford B. Anderson (Grand Rapids: Eerdmans Publishing, 2011), 366-80. In that piece, McCormack thinks Van Til does not have a correct interpretation of Immanual Kant, but McCormack does not deny that Barth's epistemology was Kantian. He also believes Van Til wrongly interpreted G*eschichte* as a realm and misunderstood revelation as historical. For another essay critical of Van Til's critique of Barth, see Gavin Ortlund, "Wholly Other or Wholly Given Over? What Van Til Missed in His Criticism of Barth," *Presbyterion* 35, no. 1 (Spring 2009): 35-52. Ortlund believes Van Til majorly misinterpreted Barth in saying that Barth did not believe in the ontological Trinity. He includes a lot of references where Barth affirms "God in himself." Ortlund accuses Van Til of not thoroughly

both interpret Barth's view of revelation to be *indirect* as opposed to direct.[279] Second, both see actualism in Barth, not only in divine/human relations but also pushed back into God's being. Actualism in God's being is where our focus will be (rather than epistemology).

The Triune Personal God

> A position is best known by the most basic distinctions that it makes. The most basic distinction of Christianity is that of God's being as self-contained, and created being as dependent upon him. Christianity is committed for better or for worse to a two-layer theory of reality or being....For the moment it is important that the basic concepts of Christianity be clearly set off from other views. And the doctrine of God's being as qualitatively distinct from every other form of being is characteristic of Christianity alone. From the Christian point of view

---

reading Barth, but ironically it seems Ortlund and not Van Til is guilty of not thoroughly reading Barth. Barth is ambiguous and therefore difficult to interpret. McCormack shows the inconsistency in Barth when he affirms a "God in himself" who would be the same whether he chose to create or not. See McCormack, *Orthodox and Modern*, 209. Concerning how thoroughly Van Til read Barth's *Church Dogmatics*, Roger Nicole gives first-hand witness to how marked up every page was in Van Til's personal copy of the *Church Dogmatics;* see Muether, *Cornelius Van Til*, 134.

[279] McCormack says, "Barth rejected the idea that revelation is *directly* given to the human knower—whether in nature, or history, or Scripture, or even in Christ. Indeed, it is finally because he believes revelation not to be directly given in Christ that Barth does not believe that it is directly given in nature, history, or Scripture. And *that* is the real sticking point between Barth and Van Til—the water's edge where the whale and the elephant meet in mutual incomprehension, each of them unable to enter the other's world and dwell. *It is in the realm of Christology that all of the issues between them come to a head.*" See McCormack, "Afterword: Reflections on Van Til's Critique of Barth," 372 (italics original).

all other forms of metaphysical theory hold to a monistic assumption.[280]

So said Van Til in the context of the doctrine of God and Christian metaphysics where he gives clear foundations in discerning Christian from non-Christian doctrine. We learned from Bavinck (chapter 4) that the first presupposition for the incarnation is the ontological Trinity who is personal, absolute, and self-complete. Van Til mirrors Bavinck in his emphasis on God's triune nature being personal, absolute, "self-complete," necessary, and unchanging.[281] The second emphasis where he mirrors his mentor is that creation is distinct from the Creator, but is also a necessary presupposition for the incarnation, as is also revelation. Trinity, creation, and revelation are all distinct for Van Til and Bavinck but are organically connected because the triune personal God who is independent (*a se*) freely created. It is important to underscore that for Van Til, the Trinity, creation, and covenant are inextricably linked. [282] God is "absolute personality," in whose triune being the unity and diversity of God are equally ultimate and correlative. [283] These are

---

[280] Van Til, *Christian Apologetics*, 30-31.

[281] For Van Til's doctrine of God, see ibid., 23-39; Van Til, *Defense of the Faith*, 30-34. For a treatment on God's names, attributes, and triunity, see Van Til, *Introduction to Systematic Theology*, 319-97.

[282] The creation doctrine is distinctly Reformed and for Van Til is connected with his doctrine of the covenant. See Muether, *Cornelius Van Til*, 127-28. Muether says concerning Van Til, "No theologian of Van Til's time had a more robust doctrine of creation or explored as fully as Van Til its covenantal character and its philosophical consequences. He often asserted that creation is the foundation stone of Reformed theology" (127).

[283] See Van Til, *Introduction to Systematic Theology*, ch. 17. For an understanding of how Van Til perceived the exhaustive relationality of the three persons in the Trinity by way of the "Representational

highlights of Van Til's Trinitarian theology which reflect Old Princeton and Old Amsterdam influences.

Van Til on McCormack's Actualism in God's Being

Van Til consistently interpreted Barth's actualism to be fundamental to his entire system. According to Van Til, Barth's actualism is anti-metaphysical and sees the "Christ event" as constitutive of God's and man's being. [284] All problems in theology are worked out "christologically" where Barth corrected the Reformers and went beyond them. There is no being of God behind the incarnate Christ, so there is no *Logos asarkos*, no eternal Son as traditionally taught. There is no "self-contained" ontological Trinity because this is not thinking christologically. That is abstract thinking which distinguishes God *in himself* from God *for us* or distinguishes the *person* of Christ from the *work* of Christ. Van Til says Barth's proposal is to think *concretely* about Christ which means as an "act." [285] We must start with Christ and not from a consideration of who God is in himself or who man is in himself.[286] Van Til clearly explains abstract vs. concrete, according to Barth, and shows how Jesus Christ is positioned in his system:

> For Barth, when we speak of Jesus Christ we must at once speak of his work as the mediator between God and man. If we spoke first of his person and then of his work, we should again be speaking of

Principle," see Lane G. Tipton, "The Triune Personal God: Trinitarian Theology in the Thought of Cornelius Van Til," 114-42.

[284] Van Til, *New Modernism*, xvii; Van Til, *Christianity and Barthianism*, 14-15.

[285] Van Til, *Christianity and Barthianism*, 13-15.

[286] Ibid., 16.

abstractions. Christ's person is identical with his work as redeemer. So also if we spoke first of his divine nature and then of his human nature, we should again be speaking of abstractions. As we cannot speak of God in himself apart from Christ, so we cannot speak of the divine nature of Christ apart from the human nature of Christ....

How then can we speak truly, that is concretely, rather than abstractly about Christ? We can do so only by speaking of him as *Act*. Abstract thinking is thinking of static entities, such as God in himself and man in himself. To think truly, that is concretely, about God is to think of him as living and therefore as acting for man in Christ. So also to think truly, that is concretely, about Christ is to think of him as the Act, or work of saving man unto God.[287]

Both Van Til and McCormack interpret Barth as teaching that God's being is actualized by the work of Jesus Christ *for us*. There is no being of God behind God's act.[288] As Van Til said about Barth's theological ontology, "God is Jesus Christ."[289] McCormack essentially says the same thing when he explains that "Jesus Christ as the One who suffers in time is what God is 'essentially.'"[290] McCormack believes Barth's mature theology is more consistently actualistic and has "been pressed back into the very being of God....God is in himself, in eternity, the mode of his Self-revelation in time—God as Jesus Christ in eternity and God as Jesus Christ in time—thus guaranteeing that the immanent Trinity and the economic Trinity will be identical in content."[291] Listen to how McCormack states what God's being is and that there is no eternal Son who is

---

[287] Ibid., 13-14 (italics original).
[288] Ibid., 44, 462.
[289] Ibid., 14, 486.
[290] McCormack, *Orthodox and Modern*, 218.
[291] Ibid.

metaphysically absolute and without flesh: "So there is no 'eternal Son' if by that is meant a mode of being in God which is not identical with Jesus Christ."[292] This line of thinking rejects the self-contained ontological Trinity and posits a god who can be known, because the Chalcedonian fathers' view of an eternal Son who is absolute and *a se* (independent) is unknown. So the eternal Son (*Logos asarkos*) is rejected by McCormack (and Barth) on new christological grounds which are based on a new doctrine of election:

> The unity here is not the unity provided by an abstract metaphysical subject; it is the concrete unity of a decision in which God gives both to himself and to humanity his and their essential being and does so with respect to one and the same figure, Jesus of Nazareth….
>
> In this view, the Reconciling Subject is no longer the Logos *simpliciter* (the abstract metaphysical subject) but the God-human in his divine-human unity. And he is this not only in time but already in eternity.[293]

By way of critique, Van Til saw in this line of thought a type of voluntarism and nominalism. McCormack actually goes beyond Barth in his doctrine of election. He believes Barth's thought carried out consistently makes the Trinity the result of God's decision to elect.[294] McCormack's correction makes God's decision the ground of the Trinity! Van Til did see Barth as a radical voluntarist/nominalist and also a realist, and with this combination there is a dialectic where God is both wholly hidden and revealed in his revelation (Jesus Christ).[295] McCormack also speaks in this

---

[292] Ibid., 219.
[293] Ibid., 228-29.
[294] See ibid., 192-96.
[295] Van Til, *Christianity and Barthianism*, 266-67.

way in describing his version of the kenosis where "the Logos does not set aside anything proper to deity, the Logos does *not* make himself directly available to putative human knowers but conceals himself in a veil of creaturely flesh."[296]

Why the rejection of the eternal Son by McCormack? One reason according to McCormack is that this eternal Son of the Chalcedonian fathers is an unknown God. He explains: "The electing God, Barth argues, is not an unknown x. He is a God whose very being—already in eternity—is determined, defined, by what God reveals himself to be in Jesus Christ, namely, a God of love and mercy towards the whole human race."[297] McCormack gives further explanation for this rejection with a quote from the *Church Dogmatics* (IV/1:52):

> If God is who and what God is in the act in which God is "with us," then we may not abstract from this act to seek a being of God above and behind this act. And because this is so, "one may not retreat here to the second 'Person' as such, to the eternal Son or the eternal Word of God *in abstracto* and, therefore, to the so-called λόγος ἄσαρκος....The second 'Person' of the Godhead in Himself and as such is not God the Reconciler. In Himself and as such, He is not revealed to us. In Himself and as such, He is precisely not *Deus pro nobis*—neither ontologically nor epistemologically."[298]

Van Til interprets Barth as saying essentially the same thing in his rejection of the eternal Son:

---

[296] McCormack, "Karl Barth's Christology as a Resource for a Reformed Version of Kenoticism," 248 (italics original).
[297] See McCormack, *Orthodox and Modern*, 189.
[298] Ibid., 220.

The Reformers, and especially Calvin, sought for God beyond Christ, as though he were not wholly revealed in Christ. For them there was some abstract, mysterious being back of Christ who arbitrarily chose some to salvation while passing others by. This created a fear and uncertainty unworthy of God and his love in Christ.[299]

Van Til sees Barth's rejection of the eternal Son as satisfying the "knowledge Beast," [300] so to speak, because this God is wholly known while he is also wholly concealed in his revelation (Jesus Christ). Kant's epistemology is seen here where, "if…the wholly unknown God is to be known at all, he must be wholly known." [301] For exhaustive knowledge to occur on Kantian soil,

the knowing subject provides the categories which order the raw stuff of the realm of pure contingency. To the extent that man knows, he, therefore, knows exhaustively. For knowledge pertains precisely to the formal relations of the world. And these formal relations originate from man himself.[302]

As man receives the information from the external world into his mind, it is his mind which provides the categories to justify his knowledge experience. The great danger Van Til saw with Barth's dialectical scheme of God being "wholly known" and "wholly unknown" in revelation is that this God has been constructed by man, the knowing subject. Is a God who is exhaustively known by man's standards the God of the Bible? Van Til answers emphatically no. How does Barth's Christ as Event or Act

---

[299] Van Til, *Christianity and Barthianism*, 15.
[300] I owe this term to K. Scott Oliphint, who has used it on occasion in the context of epistemology.
[301] Van Til, *Christianity and Barthianism*, 266.
[302] Ibid.

fit into this dialectic? According to Van Til, he "is the pinpoint of interaction between the God of pure negation and the God of pure affirmation."[303]

As we have been comparing McCormack and Van Til, certain motives or concerns have surfaced. For instance, the rejection of the eternal Son (or *Logos asarkos*) by McCormack is motivated by the concern for God to be known. Barth shared that same concern, according to Van Til. Another concern which we will now explore, as it relates to the two natures of Christ, is "suffering" and specifically "God suffering" and the "suffering" of the Son on the cross.

THE TWO NATURES OF CHRIST

Bavinck observed that the ancient heresy of patripassianism is seen in systems which are pantheistic. Bavinck critiqued the modern Christology of his day as being pantheistic. As we critique McCormack we will be asking if pantheism and patripassianism are present as well. Bavinck makes this observation:

> But in terms of its basic idea [patripassianism], it is inherent in all pantheistic systems, especially that of Hegel, Schelling, Hartmann, and others, who conceive the absolute not as being but as becoming and who allow the divine to pour itself out in the world and to finitize itself. In that case the world and humanity with all its sorrow and misery is a moment in the life of God, and the history of revelation is the history of God's suffering.[304]

---

[303] Ibid.
[304] Bavinck, *Reformed Dogmatics*, 3:275.

As we look at the "Reformed kenoticism" of Bruce McCormack we will use Bavinck and Van Til's Trinitarian theology to critique his proposal.

The Reformed Kenoticism of Bruce McCormack

> The question is not, it seems to me, whether the two-natures doctrine has a future. That much seems to have already been decided. The only real question is what form(s) it can take. So it is for the sake of an improved understanding of the potential contained in the two-natures doctrine that I offer my "Reformed" version of kenoticism.[305]

So said Bruce McCormack at the conclusion of his proposal for a "Reformed kenoticism." What is McCormack's proposal? It is an application of Barth's mature Christology (*CD* IV:1) to the kenosis doctrine found in Philippians 2:6, 7. McCormack's Reformed kenoticism does something the sixteenth- and nineteenth-century Lutheran kenoticism did not do, and that is to have a *genus tapeinotikon* (genus of humiliation) which is a communication of attributes from the human nature to the divine nature.[306] In McCormack's proposal this genus of humiliation is something that takes place not in time but in eternity in God's being.[307] God's triune being is constituted by the genus of humiliation, as McCormack explains:

> The eternal relation in which the Father "commands" and the Son "obeys" is the very relation by means of

---

[305] McCormack, "Karl Barth's Christology as a Resource for a Reformed Version of Kenoticism," 251.

[306] Ibid., 247. For an understanding of genus tapeinotikon, see Muller, *Dictionary of Latin and Greek Theological Terms*, 128.

[307] McCormack, "Karl Barth's Christology as a Resource for a Reformed Version of Kenoticism," 249-50.

which the one God freely constitutes his own being in eternity. God as "Father," Barth says is the self-positing God; God as "Son" is the self-posited God. And the Holy Spirit is that mode of being in God which "unites" Father and Son....But if the relation in which God "commands" and God "obeys" is identical with the relation which constitutes the very being of God as triune, then it is very clear that what the Son does and therefore is in time finds its ground in what he does and therefore is in eternity. What I am suggesting is that "humility" is not something added to God in his second mode of being at the point at which he assumes flesh; it *is* his second mode of being already in eternity.[308]

We must keep in mind that Barth was always concerned with the godness of God. Though he never identified himself with the Lutheran kenoticism of the nineteenth century, according to McCormack, he did believe the kenosis of Philippians 2 was an "addition" and not a "subtraction." He was deeply concerned that God remain God when he incarnates. This language of "addition" and not "subtraction" certainly sounds Reformed, but is it?

Also remember that McCormack believes holding to an eternal Son (*Logos asarkos*) makes it impossible to have an incarnation without the violation of divine immutability. So with McCormack's kenosis there is *no* "addition" of human attributes which takes place in time with a divine Logos who is absolute and complete in himself. That is how the orthodox conceived of the incarnation which resulted in an essential change in God. This new proposal conceives the kenosis (emptying) as the taking on of human attributes such as "humility" and "obedience" in eternity.[309] It is not

---

[308] Ibid., 249 (italics original).
[309] Ibid., 249-51.

that there is no incarnation in time, but that this incarnation in time "corresponds" to what has already taken place in eternity in God's being. Because God's being *is* Jesus Christ, he is fully God and fully man from all eternity, and the "Logos *as human*" is humble and obedient in time because this mirrors God's being from all eternity. [310] McCormack sees this scheme as the only way to preserve divine immutability. The orthodox are "abstract" while McCormack's Reformed kenoticism is "concrete."

What about McCormack's conception of the Trinity in light of his Reformed kenoticism? How does he define and relate God's unity to his diversity in relation to his Christology? His kenotic conception accounts for relations among the persons of the Trinity, but in following Barth he uses different terms to describe the Trinity. He holds to Barth's Trinitarian formula of "one Subject in three modes of being." [311] When McCormack considers the Hegelian proposal which *directly* identifies the second person of the Trinity as the "human Jesus," his critique is that "such an identification is certainly capable of generating *differentiation* in the divine life. What it cannot deliver is an adequate conception of *unity* in the triune life of God." He classifies this modern option as tritheistic, and does not like that it assigns the suffering of Christ to *just* the second person of the Trinity. [312] With this Hegelian scheme the Father does not suffer just like the Son, but suffers only psychologically like "an empathetic on-looker to Jesus' suffering." [313] This Hegelian scheme has the good intention of wanting a God who suffers, but it really has not achieved what it desires.

---

[310] Ibid., 247-49.
[311] Ibid., 249.
[312] Ibid., 247.
[313] Ibid.

McCormack's proposal, however, does achieve this desire of a suffering God (Father) on the cross.

Critique of McCormack's Reformed Kenoticism

Using Bavinck, this Reformed kenoticism is pantheistic and may be described as rejecting "being." It rejects God's triune being as self-complete and absolute. As Bavinck teaches, "becoming" is characteristic of creation and creatures but not God's being. McCormack's Reformed kenoticism does away with the distinction of the divine and the human and cleverly conceives God's being to be a mixture of the two natures which results in a God who can be "known" and "suffer" with us. This version of God's being is pantheistic, which, as Bavinck stated, makes God's being finite.[314] The fundamental problem Van Til saw with Barth, and is applicable to McCormack as well, is that there is no Creator/creature distinction which means their system is monistic. Van Til said, "From the Christian point of view all other forms of metaphysical theory hold to a monistic assumption." [315] Bavinck sees pantheistic systems as constituting God's being with the suffering of this world, and this is in close parallel to McCormack's construal of God's being as humble and obedient which entails the sufferings of Christ. Simply put, the human sufferings of Christ are God's being, according to McCormack.

In relation to mixing the divine and the human, Van Til saw Barth's theology making God and man correlative to each other, and McCormack's Reformed kenoticism does the same thing.[316] Van Til says it this way:

---

[314] Bavinck, *Reformed Dogmatics*, 3:275.

[315] Van Til, *Christian Apologetics*, 30-31.

[316] Van Til interpreted Barth's conception of God's being to be contemporaneous with man. He said, "God as *Geschichte* involves his

Throughout his various writings Barth has employed the concept of correlativity in order to do away with the notions of "God in Himself" and "man in himself." For all practical purposes God is nothing but that which he is in His relationship to man and man is nothing but that which he is in relationship to God. Both God and man are wholly exhausted in Christ the mediator between them....

The God and man of Barth's theology are unknown to one another till, in a common process, they become identical with one another and therefore indistinguishable from one another. Thus revelation becomes ventriloquism. The God and man of Barth's theology are non-existent till, in a common process, they become identical with one another and indistinguishable from one another. Election thus becomes their common aim and task.

Barth seeks to escape what he speaks of as the monism of traditional Reformed theology. But his own position ultimately destroys all difference between God and man by means of process. For him all reality is one stream of Becoming. This is monism with a vengeance.[317]

So, with a denial of a self-contained ontological Trinity comes a view of reality that is monistic and has no real Creator/creature distinction. They may have such a distinction but only in name.

A further concern connected with this pantheism/monism is McCormack's differentiation in the Trinity which is not adequate. He appears to have the distinctions of Father, Son, and Holy Spirit but they are in

---

contemporaneity with us. God in the fullness of his being is both wholly revealed and wholly hidden in his act of decision in Jesus Christ. God exists only in the act of his decision which is Jesus Christ. 'There is not a moment in God's being outside of this act and decision [*CD* II:1, p. 305].'" See Van Til, *Christianity and Barthianism*, 44.

[317] Van Til, *Christianity and Barthianism*, 486, 89-90.

name only. It seems this is a form of nominalism without a confession of three persons who subsist in the Godhead. He will not use the word "person" to describe the members of the Trinity because he defines a person or subject as having a separate will and mind.[318] The orthodox see the Godhead as having one will; the persons do not have separate wills, which would be tritheism. It is anathema to McCormack for only the person of the Son to incarnate. Bavinck is helpful here because he stresses that Scripture teaches it is the Son only who incarnates (John 1:14; Phil. 2:6; Heb. 2:14-15). This is why Bavinck stresses that it was the second person (with a divine nature) who incarnated and not the divine nature abstracted from the person who incarnated.[319] The latter was an impossibility for Bavinck. It seems Bavinck is wanting to make sure there is no vestige of impersonalism (as in all forms of pantheism) in an orthodox doctrine of incarnation. [320] McCormack's Reformed kenoticism may be characterized by the following categories: (1) a form of pantheism, (2) monism, (3) patripassianism, (4) a modalistic view of the Trinity, and (5) subordinationism.

We have briefly touched on each of these points except "subordinationism." We have seen that Van Til stressed the importance of starting with a proper view of God's triune nature as personal and self-contained. Without a Christian view of the Trinity, which holds that God's unity and diversity are equally ultimate, Van Til discerned that

---

[318] McCormack, "Karl Barth's Christology as a Resource for a Reformed Version of Kenoticism," 247. In *Orthodox and Modern*, 195, McCormack says, "The Second Person of the Trinity is the 'one divine I' a second time, in a different form—a form which is constituted by the anticipation of union with the humanity of Christ."
[319] Bavinck, *Reformed Dogmatics*, 3:275-6.
[320] Ibid., 3:277. Bavinck states that the incarnation would be necessary in pantheism which is indicative of an impersonal system.

modern views of the Trinity tended to emphasize either God's unity or his diversity. McCormack (following Barth) is strong on God's unity but is weak on his diversity. The Son he speaks of is Jesus Christ who is God's oneness (his being). This Son receives commands and obeys the Father from all eternity according to McCormack.[321] This trends in a subordinationist direction where the Son is essentially subordinate to the Father. Van Til's passion for the church was that it maintain a biblical Trinitarian view of God's unity and diversity with no subordinationism, which he believed was present in all heresies:

> Using the language of the one-and-many question we contend that in God the one and the many are equally ultimate. Unity in God is no more fundamental than diversity, and diversity in God is no more fundamental than unity. The persons of the Trinity are mutually exhaustive of one another. The Son and the Spirit are ontologically on a par with the Father. It is a well-known fact that all heresies in the history of the church have in some form or another taught subordinationism.[322]

VAN TIL'S CONCLUDING CONCERNS

By conceptualizing Christ, i.e. making him an event or act, Van Til saw universalism as a motive and an entailment of this Barthian construction of Christ. It was not the Christ of Chalcedon. Van Til saw Barth as eliminating all orthodox distinctions in theology from the ontological/economic Trinity, the two states of Christ, Christ's person and work, Christ's two natures, and common/special grace. He

---

[321] McCormack, "Karl Barth's Christology as a Resource for a Reformed Version of Kenoticism," 249.
[322] Van Til, *Defense of the Faith*, 48.

interpreted Barth as flattening out grace to where it is always free and sovereign.[323] And if God's being is not self-contained but is instead the "Christ event," then "Seeing Christ as *Geschichte* enables us to sense the fact that God's final word to mankind is Yes. Grace is grace for all men or it is not grace at all."[324]

CONCLUSION

Van Til was a churchman and his concern was for the health of the church and the preservation of the gospel it was commissioned to proclaim. To be fair, McCormack in his Reformed kenoticism expresses a motive for advancing his form of two natures Christology to be something that would preserve the health and life of the Reformed churches, which he sees as dying. [325] Having evaluated McCormack's Reformed kenoticism and critiqued it using Bavinck and Van Til, we are convinced it is not Reformed. As Van Til said, "the question of all questions" concerning Barthianism should be, does it have a self-contained ontological Trinity who is independent?[326] Sadly, we have seen it does not. To quote Bavinck, "Theology, if it really wants to be scriptural and Christian, cannot do better for now than to maintain the two-natures doctrine."[327] We have found McCormack's proposal not to be the form of two natures Christology that the church should follow. It is a departure from Chalcedonian orthodoxy with no clear distinction of the divine and human natures and has a faulty

---

[323] Van Til, *Christianity and Barthianism*, 13-15.
[324] Ibid., 15.
[325] McCormack, "Karl Barth's Christology as a Resource for a Reformed Version of Kenoticism," 251.
[326] Van Til, *New Modernism*, 146.
[327] Bavinck, *Reformed Dogmatics*, 3:304.

view of the Trinity. Of all that Van Til teaches us, it is that "in the Reformed Faith the freedom of God, the self-contained God, is central to everything." When this is lost there is no gospel to proclaim.[328]

---

[328] Ibid., 3:490.

CHAPTER 6

CONCLUSION

We have been exploring the Barthian Christology of Bruce McCormack in order to see if it is Chalcedonian. We first looked at McCormack's exposition of Barth's Christology to learn of its unique features. The early Barth, according to McCormack, was less consistent in applying "actualism" to his theology. As Barth matured he showed less of a Greek essentialism and a more thoroughly actualistic theological ontology. Barth's revision of the doctrine of election is a watershed moment where Barth registered the correction that Jesus Christ is not only the object of election but also the subject of election. It is in this primal decision *for us* where God assigns the being he will have for all eternity. For Barth, God's being is Jesus Christ. From *CD* II/2— where this revision of election occurs—forward, Barth's actualizing/historicizing of God's being is consistently applied to his Christology (in *CD* IV/1-3). The terminology of one person and two natures is still retained, but the concept of "history" is now inserted into both Christ's person and his natures. This mature Barthian Christology has thoroughly rejected any traditional way of defining substance/nature. So, the content of these terms (person and natures) has been redefined by actualizing them.

According to McCormack, this redefining of the Chalcedonian categories of person and natures eliminates the problem of divine immutability which was Barth's lifelong concern (the "red thread" running throughout his theology). Barth was convinced the orthodox view of an unchanging Logos who then takes on flesh in time had undergone an essential change. This problem of an essential change in time is eliminated by the rejection of the eternal Son of God (*Logos asarkos*) who is replaced with Jesus Christ who is the God-man from all eternity.

In chapter 2 we established what Chalcedonian Christology is by briefly expositing the Christology of Charles Hodge of Old Princeton. Hodge, we saw, consistently used the human analogy of man's makeup of body and soul in one person to illustrate the Chalcedonian boundaries of one person and two distinct natures (divine and human). The concept of substance is critical to maintaining a proper understanding of Christ's two natures. We learned there must be a distinction of Christ's two natures while maintaining a real personal union of those natures which occurs in the one person of Christ. Hodge affirms it was the eternal Logos who assumed a real human body and soul in time. The passages which most explicitly teach this are John 1:1-14 and Philippians 2:6-8. Scripture also teaches that it is Christ's one person who works from both natures, though he is named by one of the natures or both of them.

In chapter 3 we compared and contrasted Hodge's Christology to McCormack's in these four areas: (1) creeds, (2) Christ's two natures, (3) Creator/creature distinction, and (4) philosophy. Both affirm creeds as valuable but there is a different attitude toward creedalism. McCormack's attitude is similar to the modern Christology of Hodge's day which ignored the clear teaching of the creeds or looked for ways to retain the formal wording but make substantial changes to the language. McCormack's Christology has a formal similarity to that of Hodge with Christ being "truly divine" and "truly human," but what those terms mean has been drastically changed. McCormack affirms a Creator/creature distinction, but with his rejection of substance there are no divine or human substances. There is a third thing (*tertium quid*) which is the God-man from all eternity which is God's being. Regarding philosophy, both men see value in using it but it seems to be driving McCormack's theological project whereas Hodge uses it as a servant. For Hodge, God and Scripture are the two *principia* (foundations).

In chapter 4 we compared and contrasted McCormack's Christology with that of Herman Bavinck of Old Amsterdam. We saw Bavinck's unique contribution to Chalcedonian Christology to be his emphasis on the ontological Trinity, creation, and revelation as the foundations for the incarnation of the eternal Son in time. Bavinck underscored the Reformed distinctive of the triune God's personal consciousness. God as the absolute, self-complete Trinity is the root for the incarnation, and because this absolutely personal God has decreed all things from eternity the incarnation is not an afterthought for God. It was part of his eternal plan and something he *freely* did, and was not borne out of necessity as it is with modern Christology which is pantheistic and impersonal. God is relational because he is *absolute personal self consciousness*, and while he is self-complete and independent he has chosen from eternity to relate to his creation by way of covenant. The mediator of the covenant, the eternal Son, knew from all eternity that he would become incarnate in time.

McCormack's Christology was compared and contrasted with Bavinck's in these four areas: (1) theological ontology, (2) one person in Christ, (3) two natures in Christ, and (4) divine immutability. McCormack's charge that the orthodox conception of one divine person working out of two natures is Nestorian was addressed, and Bavinck's stress on the distinction of persons of the Trinity was helpful. Because Bavinck has a Creator/creature distinction where the divine is uncreated, independent, and *a se,* and the creature is becoming and dependent, he taught that the eternal Logos was greater than the human nature and worked through it. McCormack would see the two natures (divine and human) as equal. Bavinck emphasized it was the second person of the Trinity who was incarnated and that the natures were not abstractly united. It was a personal union of the eternal Son with a human nature. McCormack's second concern of immutability was also looked at using Bavinck's insights. Bavinck would see any mixing of the two natures (such as McCormack has done) to be a violation of immutability.

Our final stop, chapter 5, was with Cornelius Van Til in critiquing the Reformed kenoticism of McCormack, which is his form of a two natures Christology. We continued to use Bavinck's insights as well. Van Til's emphasis was on the self-contained, triune, personal God and the Creator/creature distinction. We must start here and not compromise our doctrine of God because all heresies in the history of the church have had some type of subordinationism in God's being.

We spent some time comparing Van Til's interpretation of Barth with McCormack's. I am convinced they are similar in two fundamental areas: (1) God's being is actualized, and (2) revelation is indirect. Our comparison focused on the actualization of God's being which entails a rejection of the *Logos asarkos.*

We looked at McCormack's Reformed kenoticism which teaches that the Son's self-emptying (kenosis) happened in eternity. This kenosis constitutes God's being where God's being suffers and is humble and obedient. The *genus tapeinoticum* (genus of humility) which transfers attributes from the human to the divine is done by God's election in Jesus Christ in eternity. Van Til's critique shows this Reformed kenoticism to be unorthodox because it rejects God as independent and self-contained. McCormack's Reformed kenoticism is characterized by the following categories: (1) a form of pantheism, (2) monism, (3) patripassianism, (4) a modalistic view of the Trinity, (5) Eutychianism, and (6) subordinationism. It does not teach a distinction of the divine and the human natures so it has no adequate Creator/creature distinction.

My thesis is that the Barthian Christology of Bruce McCormack is not Chalcedonian because it rejects the eternal Son (*Logos asarkos*). The church needs to follow the Chalcedonian Christology of Hodge, Bavinck, and Van Til because what is at stake in these conversations is the gospel. As Van Til said, if the free, independent, self-contained triune God is rejected there is no gospel to preach.

BIBLIOGRAPHY

Barth, Karl. *Church Dogmatics*. Vol. 4, *The Doctrine of Reconciliation*. Edited by G. W. Bromiley and T. F. Torrance. Translated by T. H. L. Parker, W. B Johnston, Harold Knight, and J. L. M. Haire. London: T&T Clark International, 2004.

Bavinck, Herman. *Reformed Dogmatics*. Vol. 2, *God and Creation*. Edited by John Bolt. Translated by John Vriend. Grand Rapids: Baker Academic, 2004.

———. *Reformed Dogmatics*. Vol. 3, *Sin and Salvation in Christ*. Edited by John Bolt. Translated by John Vriend. Grand Rapids: Baker Academic, 2006.

Beeke, Joel R., and Mark Jones. *A Puritan Theology: Doctrine for Life*. Grand Rapids: Reformation Heritage Books, 2012.

Berkhof, Louis. *The History of Christian Doctrine*. 1937. Reprint, Edinburgh: Banner of Truth Trust, 2009.

Calhoun, David B. *Princeton Seminary*. Vol. 1, *Faith and Learning, 1812-1868*. Edinburgh: The Banner of Truth Trust, 1994.

————. *Princeton Seminary*. Vol. 2, *The Majestic Testimony, 1869-1929*. Edinburgh: The Banner of Truth Trust, 1996.

Cassidy, James J. "No 'Absolute Impeccability': Charles Hodge and Christology at Old and New Princeton." *The Confessional Presbyterian* 9 (2013): 143-56.

Dempsey, Michael T. *Trinity and Election in Contemporary Theology*. Grand Rapids: Eerdmans, 2011.

Frame, John M. *Cornelius Van Til: An Analysis of His Thought*. Phillipsburg, NJ: P&R Publishing, 1995.

Gaffin, Richard B. Jr. *Resurrection and Redemption: A Study in Paul's Soteriology*. 2nd ed. Phillipsburg, NJ: P&R Publishing, 1987.

Gleason, Ron. *Herman Bavinck: Pastor, Churchman, Statesman, and Theologian*. Phillipsburg, NJ: P&R Publishing, 2010.

Hanson, R. P. C. *The Search for the Christian Doctrine of God: The Arian Controversy, 318-381*. Edinburgh: T&T Clark, 1988.

Helseth, Paul Kjoss. *"Right Reason" and the Princeton Mind: An Unorthodox Proposal*. Phillipsburg, NJ: P&R Publishing, 2010.

Hodge, A. A. *The Life of Charles Hodge*. Edinburgh: The Banner of Truth Trust, 2010.

————. *Outlines of Theology*. 1878. Reprint, Edinburgh: The Banner of Truth Trust, 1999.

————. *The Westminster Confession: A Commentary*. 1869. Reprint, Edinburgh: The Banner of Truth Trust, 2002.

Hodge, Charles. *A Commentary on Ephesians*. 1856. Reprint, Edinburgh: The Banner of Truth Trust, 1991.

————. *A Commentary on Romans.* 1864. Reprint, Edinburgh: The Banner of Truth Trust, 1997.

————. *Systematic Theology.* 3 vols. 1871-1873. Reprint, Grand Rapids: Eerdmans, 1995.

Helm, Paul. "John Calvin and the Hiddenness of God." In *Engaging the Doctrine of God: Contemporary Protestant Perspectives,* edited by Bruce L. McCormack, 67-82. Grand Rapids: Baker Academic, 2008.

Hunsinger, George. *How to Read Karl Barth: The Shape of His Theology.* New York: Oxford University Press, 1991.

————. "Karl Barth's Christology: Its Basic Chalcedonian Character." In *The Cambridge Companion to Karl Barth,* edited by John Webster, 127-42. Cambridge: Cambridge University Press, 2000.

McCormack, Bruce L. "The Actuality of God: Karl Barth in Conversation with Open Theism." In *Engaging the Doctrine of God: Contemporary Protestant Perspectives,* edited by Bruce L. McCormack, 185-242. Grand Rapids: Baker Academic, 2008.

————. "The Being of Holy Scripture Is in Becoming: Karl Barth in Conversation with American Evangelical Criticism." In *Evangelicals & Scripture: Tradition, Authority and Hermeneutics,* edited by Vincent Bacote, Laura C. Miguelez, and Dennis L. Okholm, 55-75. Downers Grove, IL: Inter Varsity Press, 2004.

————. "Divine Impassibility or Simply Divine Constancy? Implications of Karl Barth's Later Christology for Debates over Impassibility." In *Divine Impassibility and the Mystery of Human Suffering,* edited by James F. Keating and Thomas Joseph White, O.P., 150-86. Grand Rapids: Eerdmans, 2009.

————. "Karl Barth's Christology as a Resource for a Reformed Version of Kenoticism." *International Journal of Systematic Theology* 8, no. 3 (July 2006): 243-51.

————. *Karl Barth's Critically Realistic Dialectical Theology: Its Genesis and Development, 1909-1936*. Oxford: Oxford University Press, 1995.

————. "The Ontological Presuppositions of Barth's Doctrine of the Atonement." In *The Glory of the Atonement: Biblical Historical and Practical Perspectives*, edited by Charles E. Hill and Frank A. James III, 346-66. Downers Grove, IL: Inter Varsity Press, 2004.

————. *Orthodox and Modern*. Grand Rapids: Baker Academic, 2008.

McCormack, Bruce L., and Clifford B. Anderson, eds. *Karl Barth and American Evangelicalism*. Grand Rapids: Eerdmans, 2011.

Muether, John R. *Cornelius Van Til: Reformed Apologist and Churchman*. Phillipsburg, NJ: P&R Publishing, 2008.

Muller, Richard A. *Dictionary of Latin and Greek Theological Terms: Drawn Principally From Protestant Scholastic Theology*. Grand Rapids: Baker Academic, 1995.

Murray, John. *The Epistle to the Romans: The English Text with Introduction, Exposition and Notes*. Grand Rapids: Eerdmans, 1997.

Noll, Mark. *America's God: From Jonathan Edwards to Abraham Lincoln*. Oxford: Oxford University Press, 2002.

————, ed. *The Princeton Theology, 1812-1921: Scripture, Science, and Theological Method from Archibald Alexander to Benjamin Warfield*. Grand Rapids: Baker Academic, 2001.

Oliphint, K. Scott. "Bavinck's Realism, The Logos Principle, and Sola Scriptura." *Westminster Theological Journal* 72, no. 2 (2010): 359-90.

———. *God With Us: Divine Condescension and the Attributes of God.* Wheaton, IL: Crossway, 2012.

———. *Reasons for Faith: Philosophy in the Service of Theology.* Phillipsburg, NJ: P&R Publishing, 2006.

Ortlund, Gavin. "Wholly Other or Wholly Given Over? What Van Til Missed in His Criticism of Barth." *Presbyterion* 35, no. 1 (Spring 2009): 35-52.

Schaff, Philip, and David S. Schaff, eds. *The Creeds of Christendom: With a History and Critical Notes.* Vol. 1. Grand Rapids: Baker Books, 2007.

Tipton, Lane G. "The Presence of Divine Persons: Extending the Incarnational Analogy to Impeccability and Inerrancy." *The Confessional Presbyterian* 6 (2010): 196-201.

———."The Triune Personal God: Trinitarian Theology in the Thought of Cornelius Van Til." PhD diss., Westminster Theological Seminary, 2004.

Van Til, Cornelius. *Christianity and Barthianism.* Phillipsburg, NJ: P&R Publishing, 1962.

———. *Common Grace and the Gospel.* Phillipsburg, NJ: P&R Publishing, 1972.

———. *The Defense of the Faith.* 3rd ed. Phillipsburg, NJ: Presbyterian and Reformed Publishing Co., 1967.

———. *An Introduction to Systematic Theology: Prolegomena and the Doctrines of Revelation, Scripture, and God.* Edited by William Edgar. 2nd ed. Phillipsburg, NJ: P&R Publishing, 2007.

————. "Nature and Scripture" in *The Infallible Word: A Symposium by the Members of the Faculty of Westminster Theological Seminary*. Edited by N. B. Stonehouse and Paul Woolley. 2nd ed. Phillipsburg, NJ: P&R Publishing, 2002.

————. *The New Modernism: An Appraisal of the Theology of Barth and Brunner*. Philadelphia: Presbyterian and Reformed Publishing Co., 1947.

————. *A Survey of Christian Epistemology*. Phillipsburg, NJ: Presbyterian and Reformed Publishing Co., n.d.

Vos, Geerhardus. *Redemptive History and Biblical Interpretation: The Shorter Writings of Geerhardus Vos*. Edited by Richard B. Gaffin Jr. Phillipsburg: P&R Publishing, 1980.

Made in the USA
Middletown, DE
05 May 2021

39088796R00080